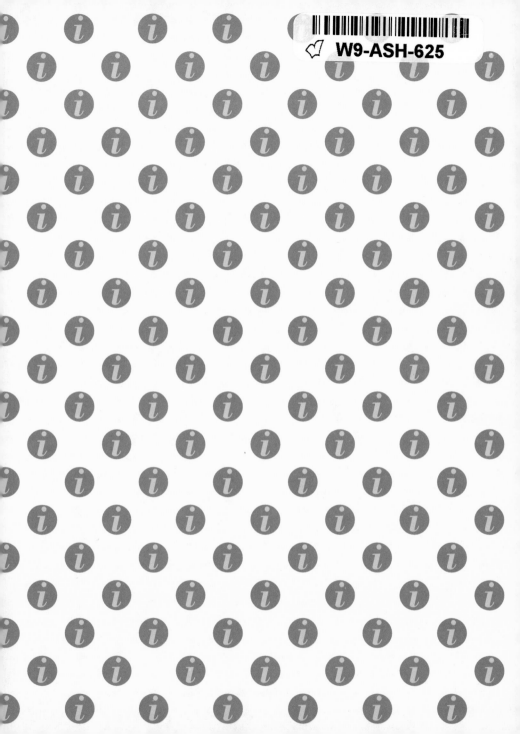
W9-ASH-625

IDENTIFYING
PALMS

The new compact study guide and identifier

Martin Gibbons

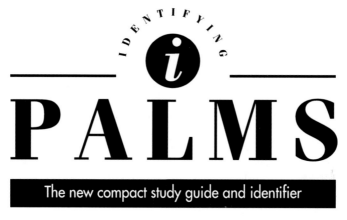

PALMS

The new compact study guide and identifier

Martin Gibbons

CHARTWELL
BOOKS, INC.

A QUINTET BOOK

Published by Chartwell Books
A Division of Book Sales, Inc.
PO Box 7100
Edison, New Jersey 08818-7100

This edition produced for sale
in the U.S.A., its territories
and dependencies only.

Copyright © 1993 Quintet Publishing Limited.
All rights reserved. No part of this publication may be
reproduced, stored in a retrieval system or transmitted in
any form or by any means, electronic, mechanical,
photocopying, recording or otherwise, without the
permission of the copyright holder.

Reprinted 1995

ISBN 1-55521-837-7

This book was designed and produced by
Quintet Publishing Limited
6 Blundell Street
London N7 9BH

Project Editor: Laura Sandelson
Creative Director: Richard Dewing
Designers: Nicky Chapman, Stuart Walden
Editor: Diana Brinton

Typeset in Great Britain by
Central Southern Typesetters, Eastbourne
Manufactured in Singapore by
J. Film Process Singapore Pte. Ltd
Printed in Singapore by
Star Standard Industries Pte. Ltd

CONTENTS

INTRODUCTION

Palms form an integral and important part of the vegetation of the tropics and subtropics, and there are some 3,800 known species. Not all grow either in deserts or on white, sandy shorelines, as is popularly supposed. The great majority grow deep in the gloomy rainforest and perhaps never see the sun, certainly not as young plants. It is for this reason that many species can adapt to life as house plants, and some will tolerate even quite deep shade.

Further, there are many species that grow a long way from the tropics, and it comes as a surprise to many people to discover that, far from needing heat and humidity to grow well, a good number of palms actually prefer cool climates, and will thrive outdoor in temperate areas.

Many species of palm are difficult even for the experts to identify, since they differ only in flower or pollen details. However, most of the palms that are more commonly encountered are relatively easy to tell apart, having major, often unique, characteristics which, with guidance, enable amateur and professional plant spotters alike to tell the difference. It is on these species that this book concentrates, and it is hoped that it will prove not only a useful guide, but a means of adding to the enjoyment on any vacation or business trip to the tropics. Each species is illustrated in color, and the text provides recognition pointers to the main characteristics of the palm – its overall height, origin, leaf shape, trunk size and so on – so that, with these in mind, recognition should be quite easy.

Since travel is much more common than in days gone by, more and more people from temperate climes are developing an interest in tropical and subtropical plants in general, and in palms in particular. Many people like to grow palms, either in their home or greenhouse, or – if they are lucky enough to live in a warm climate – their yard. It is hoped that this book will prove of practical use to all readers, as both the indoor and outdoor cultivation requirements of each species are discussed.

The International Palm Society is an organization dedicated to those interested in palms, and members receive a quarterly magazine *Principes*, in which they can read and learn about these fascinating plants. The society's address is PO Box 368, Lawrence, Kansas 66044, USA. In Europe, the European Palm Society caters for palm enthusiasts with a specific interest in the more cold-hardy species, and those that prefer temperate conditions. Their color magazine *Chamaerops*, also a quarterly, can be obtained from The Palm Centre, 563 Upper Richmond Road West, London SW14 7ED, UK.

LEFT The Parlor palm has been underwatered. It also carries the symptoms of red spider mite – light brown patches on the edges and eventually over the whole of some leaves. Daily mist spraying acts as a preventative, since it keeps up the humidity.

CULTIVATION

INDOOR PALMS

Many palms that are available as house plants need only the minimum of care and attention to thrive; others are perhaps more difficult, but then again, perhaps more rewarding. Like other houseplants, palms need certain conditions, and these are considered under the following categories – light, temperature, water, humidity, feed.

LIGHT The majority of palms for indoor use require bright, indirect light. Direct sunlight through glass, especially during the summer months, can scorch the leaves of the plant and eventually kill it, though this is not a problem during winter, when your palm should be positioned to take the best advantage of whatever light is available. Plants can either be protected from direct sunlight with screens, blinds or shades, or perhaps be positioned in a window which gets no direct sunlight.

Some palms can tolerate quite low light. These include the Lady palm (*Rhapis excelsa*), the Pygmy date palm (*Phoenix roebelenii*) and the Fishtail palm (*Caryota mitis*). It must be admitted, however, that although these plants will put up with low light, they do better in brighter conditions, and it may be advisable to move them to a brighter spot for about one week in every three. Many house palms can be stood outside during the warmer months of the year, when they will benefit from being placed in dappled shade.

TEMPERATURE A palm's requirements as to temperature can be guessed at from its origin. Is it from the tropics? If so, it will almost certainly require warm conditions to thrive, though it is sometimes surprising what cool conditions some tropical palms will put up with, and even thrive in. Is it from desert regions (a date palm, a Brahea, or a Washingtonia, for example)? If so, it will require hot, dry and bright conditions, but will also be able to tolerate very cold temperatures, for short periods. Some palms can put up with temperatures well below freezing, and the hardiest of these (such as Trachycarpus or Chamaerops) make wonderful specimens for the garden, even in temperate zones.

WATER This is without doubt the subject that causes most concern among house plant owners, who are equally terrified of over- and under-watering. The answer is simple; let the surface of the soil dry out slightly, and then give the soil a thorough soak. *Don't* give the palm a little water every day. *Don't* let your palm stand in water, and *don't* let the soil remain waterlogged. *Do* allow the surface of the soil to dry out first. *Do* give a thorough soak to the soil, ideally by immersion if the plant is manageable. If the soil becomes too dry, it will shrink away from the edges of the pot; when water is applied, it will run around the soil instead

ABOVE All palms, like the Kentia *are extremely sensitive to chemicals. Leaves should always be cleaned with a damp sponge, never a chemical cleaner.*

of through it, and the water appearing in the saucer below may be taken as an indication that the plant has had enough. Not so! Immerse the plant to correct this condition.

HUMIDITY As with light, the origin of the palm can be a guide as to its humidity requirements. Small delicate tropical palms will obviously require a humid atmosphere; plants from the desert will not. Interestingly, palms can be surprisingly adaptable, and new leaves grown in a drier atmosphere will be more tolerant of dry air than those on the same plant which grew in the tropics. Use a hand mister often − as often as you like. Install an electric humidifier which will benefit the plants as well as furniture, paintings, and indeed the human inhabitants. In a greenhouse or conservatory, splash water about liberally in summer; in winter, open the windows to allow fresh, humid air to enter from time to time.

FEED There are now many proprietary brands of house-plant fertilizer on the market, and most of these will be fine for your palms. Spring is the time to begin giving fertilizer to your palms, according to the manufacturer's instructions, perhaps once a week, or once every two weeks, or maybe with every watering. Don't over-fertilize potted palms, as this is one of the causes of browning leaf tips.

CARYOTA

TRACHYCARPUS

CHAMEADOREA

CHRYSALIDOCARPUS

Shown here are the main varieties of palms. They fall into two main divisions – those with pinnate (feathery) fronds and those with palmate (fan-like) ones.

HOWEA

RHAPIS

PHOENIX

LYTOCARPUM

OUTDOOR PALMS

If you have the climate and the space, then growing palms outdoors is the ideal way to enjoy these wonderful plants. What you can grow obviously depends on where you live; those near the equator have a much larger choice, of course, but even in temperate regions such as Britain and the northern United States there are still several possibilities. Even here, the range can be increased if you are prepared to protect your palms in the colder weather.

Consider long and hard before planting a palm on your property. What goes in as a small seedling, can grow to a huge and overpowering tree in perhaps just a few years. Some palms grow very quickly, especially in the tropics, and can completely dominate their surroundings in a remarkably short time. However, unlike most other trees, their ultimate shape and size is totally predictable. In temperate countries, this problem is less acute, but is still a consideration.

Palms have relatively fine roots, and are not a danger to walls, drains and foundations. They can be planted quite close to walls, from which they will then lean out in characteristic fashion.

Be careful with your choice of palms – many are primadonnas, demanding a central position and lots of attention. Too many of these near each other will create confusion and lack of balance. It is preferable to have one or two main subjects, with perhaps a few smaller palms for under-planting. Palms grow well with yuccas, cordylines, bamboos and pines, and a mixed group can look very effective.

PLANTING OUT Your palm will probably go in as a small seedling. Having given due consideration to the above, dig a hole, perhaps putting in some good top-soil, or compost, and position the new arrival. Planting your seedling at the bottom of a saucer-shaped depression will facilitate watering. For the first few years – until well established – most palms will require protection from too much sun, especially in hot climates. This can be achieved in a variety of ways, including shade netting. Dappled sunlight is fine.

Water well for the first few weeks, until active growth is noticed. Thereafter, the plant's requirements will differ according to its original habitat. Generally speaking, well-drained soil, an abundance of water (especially in dry weather) and adequate fertilizing will supply all its needs. Large palms need a lot of fertilizing, and an annual top dressing with stable manure, or well-rotted compost will work wonders.

Your palm may arrive as an established tree, either in rootball form or in a tub. Don't underestimate the weight of a large palm. Any palm with more than a couple of feet of stout trunk will require lifting tackle, or perhaps a small crane, to move it safely. A date palm, for instance, with just a yard of trunk, will weigh almost a ton. Prepare the planting site well in advance, and the palm can be delivered straight to the hole.

Again, water liberally until new growth is observed; this is an indication that new roots will have formed, and the watering can be eased. However, a newly planted palm, whatever its size, should never be allowed to dry out, and should not be given fertilizer for twelve months.

Garden palms require little in the way of maintenance, just the removal of old dead leaves which, if not shed cleanly by the particular species, need to be trimmed off, with a saw or secateurs.

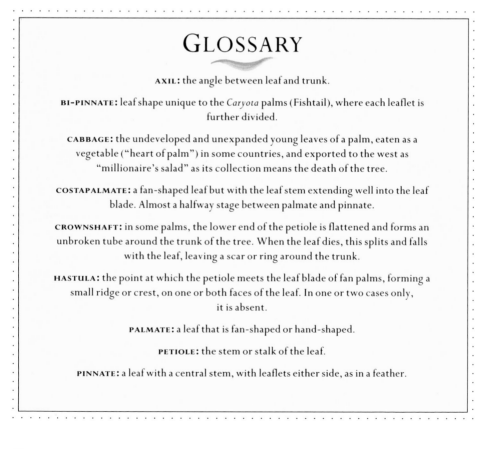

GLOSSARY

AXIL: the angle between leaf and trunk.

BI-PINNATE: leaf shape unique to the *Caryota* palms (Fishtail), where each leaflet is further divided.

CABBAGE: the undeveloped and unexpanded young leaves of a palm, eaten as a vegetable ("heart of palm") in some countries, and exported to the west as "millionaire's salad" as its collection means the death of the tree.

COSTAPALMATE: a fan-shaped leaf but with the leaf stem extending well into the leaf blade. Almost a halfway stage between palmate and pinnate.

CROWNSHAFT: in some palms, the lower end of the petiole is flattened and forms an unbroken tube around the trunk of the tree. When the leaf dies, this splits and falls with the leaf, leaving a scar or ring around the trunk.

HASTULA: the point at which the petiole meets the leaf blade of fan palms, forming a small ridge or crest, on one or both faces of the leaf. In one or two cases only, it is absent.

PALMATE: a leaf that is fan-shaped or hand-shaped.

PETIOLE: the stem or stalk of the leaf.

PINNATE: a leaf with a central stem, with leaflets either side, as in a feather.

HOW TO USE THIS BOOK

This book is laid out so as to give the maximum amount of information in
the clearest possible way. The introduction contains general hints and
advice on plant care, which is amplified in the identifier section of the
book. This deals individually with a wide variety of indoor and outdoor
palms. Arranged alphabetically, each entry contains a picture of the palm
with its family or genus name and common name, information about its
distinguishing characteristics, cultivation habits and an easy care guide.
The symbols given below accompany each entry and are intended to give
vital information about the size of the palm, the leaf shape and trunk
at a glance.

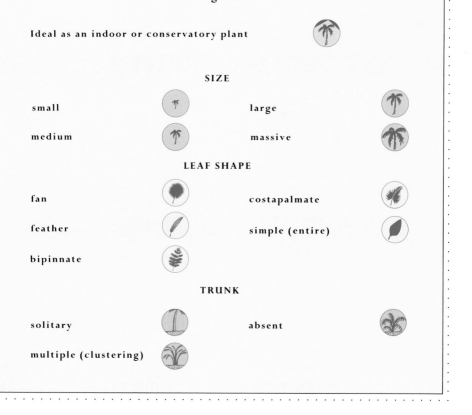

Ideal as an indoor or conservatory plant

SIZE

small

large

medium

massive

LEAF SHAPE

fan

costapalmate

feather

simple (entire)

bipinnate

TRUNK

solitary

absent

multiple (clustering)

PALM IDENTIFIER

ACOELORRHAPHE WRIGHTII (SYN. PAUROTIS WRIGHTII)
SILVER SAW PALMETTO

An unmistakable clumping palm, usually with a few taller trunks dominating the rest, the silver saw palmetto is much used in Florida for street and park decoration.

ORIGIN Central America, West Indies and Florida.
MATURE HEIGHT To 15 or 20ft.
TRUNK Multiple, slender, covered with brown fiber.
LEAF Fan-shaped, with silver back.
FLOWER STALK From among the leaves.
FRUIT Small and round, black when ripe.
SEED Small, round.
CULTIVATION The seeds germinate rapidly and easily. *OUTDOORS* A palm for the tropics and subtropics, it is widely cultivated. It prefers damp soil, or at least access to permanent underground moisture. *INDOORS* Little is known about its use as an indoor plant.

AIPHANES EROSA
MACAW PALM

An interesting palm, it is covered in sharp spines from an early age, which should be taken into account when choosing an outdoor site.

ORIGIN West Indies.
MATURE HEIGHT To 15ft.
TRUNK Slim, solitary, dark, covered in fine sharp black spines.
LEAF Pinnate, with long leaflets, held flat; the petiole and, to an extent, the underparts of the leaf, are also spiny.
FLOWER STALK From among the leaf bases; fragrant, creamy flowers.
FRUIT Red when ripe.
SEED Small and round, distinctively pitted on the surface.
CULTIVATION The seeds germinate easily if fresh. *OUTDOORS* The Macaw palm is an attractive small tree for the tropics and subtropics. *INDOORS* Certainly suitable for a moist conservatory, it would make an interesting addition to any collection.

ARCHONTOPHOENIX
ALEXANDRAE
ALEXANDER PALM, KING PALM

A beautiful, easily cultivated and popular palm, the Alexander or king palm is commonly seen in the tropics and subtropics.
ORIGIN Eastern Australia.
MATURE HEIGHT To 60ft.
TRUNK Solitary, light gray, covered with old leaf scars, often swollen at the base; mid-green crownshaft.
LEAF Pinnate, held flat, sometimes twisted so it is perpendicular to the ground; the underside of the leaflet is silvery – a key identification factor.
FLOWER STALK From below the crownshaft, cream color.
FRUIT Round, ¾in in diameter, red when ripe. Borne in huge numbers.
SEED Covered in longitudinal fibers.
CULTIVATION The seeds germinate within a few weeks, and subsequent seedling growth is also fast. *OUTDOORS* Fast-growing, the king palm is cultivated in tropics and subtropics. *INDOORS* This may be cultivated indoors, but requires high levels of light and humidity.

ARCHONTOPHOENIX
CUNNINGHAMIANA
BANGALOW PALM

A common and popular, slender pinnate palm, it is similar to
A. alexandrae in appearance.
ORIGIN Eastern Australia.
MATURE HEIGHT To 60 or 70ft.
TRUNK Slim, gray, with old leaf scars, mid-green crownshaft.
LEAF Pinnate, mid-green, but without the silvery undersides of
A. alexandrae.
FLOWER STALK From below the the crownshaft, violet color.
FRUIT Small, red when ripe, and borne in huge numbers.
SEED Covered in longitudinal fibers.
CULTIVATION The fibrous seeds germinate easily and quickly.
OUTDOORS An easy outdoor palm for tropics, subtropics and warm temperate climates, it shows some tolerance to cold and will take a few degrees of frost. It is also fast-growing. *INDOORS* The bangalow palm requires good light and humidity, but can be grown indoors.

ARECA CATECHU
BETEL NUT PALM

A familiar and attractive palm in the tropics, it is commonly grown for its seed – the betel nut, which is a mild narcotic.
ORIGIN Southeast Asia.
MATURE HEIGHT To 50ft.
TRUNK Solitary, distinctly ringed, with crownshaft.
LEAF Broad leaflets, or sometimes broad and narrow on the same leaf, the tips being jagged.
FLOWER STALK From below the crownshaft.
FRUIT Red when ripe, to 2in long.
SEED Oval, but flattened at one end, it is chewed, in tropical countries, with other ingredients, as a mild stimulant.
CULTIVATION The large seeds germinate quickly if fresh, and subsequent growth is also fast. *OUTDOORS* An excellent palm for the tropics and subtropics, it prefers a shady location, and plenty of water. *INDOORS* The betel nut palm requires warmth and humidity, but may successfully be cultivated indoors. Plants are sometimes sold in plant centers as "Mini Cocos."

ARECA IPOT

Although not dissimilar to *A. catechu,* it is smaller and daintier.
ORIGIN The Philippines.
MATURE HEIGHT To 12 or 15ft.
TRUNK Solitary, distinctly ringed, with swollen crownshaft.
LEAF A mixture of wide and narrow leaflets on the one leaf; the ends of the leaflets look as though chewed by some animal.
FLOWER STALK From below the crownshaft.
FRUIT Red when ripe, to 2in long.
SEED Oval, but flattened at one end.
CULTIVATION The large seeds germinate quickly if fresh, and subsequent growth is fast. *OUTDOORS* An excellent palm for the tropics and subtropics, it prefers a shady location, with an abundance of water in dry weather. *INDOORS* If warmth and humidity can be provided, it may be successfully grown indoors.

ARECA TRIANDRA

An attractive clumping palm for the moist tropics, where it is commonly grown.
ORIGIN Malaysia and India.
MATURE HEIGHT To 15ft.
TRUNK Multiple, distinctly ringed, with crownshafts.
LEAF Wide and narrow leaflets are often found on the same leaf, the tips being jagged.
FLOWER STALK From below the crownshaft.
FRUIT Orange/red when ripe, to 1in long.
SEED Oval, but flattened at one end.
CULTIVATION The large seeds germinate quickly if fresh, and subsequent growth is fast. *OUTDOORS* Another excellent palm for the tropics and subtropics, it prefers a position out of direct sunlight, and plenty of water. *INDOORS A. triandra* requires warmth and humidity, but indoor cultivation may be successful.

ARECA VESTIARIA

An attractive small-to-medium palm, it is most notable for its orange crownshaft, a feature which easily distinguishes it from all other *Arecas,* and most other palms.
ORIGIN Indonesia.
MATURE HEIGHT To 30ft.
TRUNK Solitary, slim, sometimes seen with stilt roots; it has a crownshaft, which is bright orange in color.
LEAF Typical *Areca* feather-shaped leaf.
FLOWER STALK From below the crownshaft.
FRUIT Orange in color when ripe, 1in long.
SEED Oval, flattened at one end.
CULTIVATION This is easily grown from seed, which germinates readily, and plants can be quite fast-growing. *OUTDOORS* A palm for the tropics and subtropics, *A. vestiaria* is an excellent addition to any collection. *INDOORS* It is not known to have been tried indoors.

ARENGA ENGLERI

This attractive small palm grows well in climates ranging from tropical to temperate, and will even take some frost.
ORIGIN Taiwan.
MATURE HEIGHT To 10ft.
TRUNK Multiple, short, covered with old leaf fibers.
LEAF The long, broad, pinnate leaf is green above, silvery below; there are long, narrow leaflets, often with irregular edges and tips.
FLOWER STALK From among the leaves; that particular stem dying after fruiting.
FRUIT Round, ½in in diameter, dark red when ripe. The pulp is caustic and should not be handled without gloves.
SEED There are two or three per fruit, with corresponding flat sides.
CULTIVATION The seeds are erratic to germinate, some sprouting within a few weeks, others taking months. *OUTDOORS* Plants grow slowly to a broad, bushy shape, much wider than tall. This palm is cold-tolerant, so worth a try in cooler climates, where it is very slow-growing. It can be planted in either sun or shade. *INDOORS* This has not been tested for indoor use, and is probably not suitable.

ARENGA PINNATA
SUGAR PALM

This large, towering, untidy palm is cultivated for its sugary sap.
ORIGIN Southeast Asia.
MATURE HEIGHT To 60ft or more.
TRUNK Solitary, 12in in diameter, covered with old leaf bases and black dusty fibers, with spines 3in or 4in long.
LEAF Long, pinnate, erect, with long narrow leaflets, dark green above, silvery beneath.
FLOWER STALK When the tree has reached maturity, the first inflorescence appears in the highest leaf axil, subsequent flower stalks appearing lower and lower down the tree. When the final one has produced flowers and seeds, the tree dies.
FRUIT Round, dark red to purple, 1½in in diameter; the fruit pulp should not be handled.
SEED Usually three per fruit, flat-sided to fit.
CULTIVATION Sugar palms are easily grown from seed, which germinates quickly. *OUTDOORS* Fast-growing in the tropics, they are slower in cooler areas and are not ideal for decorative purposes, firstly because of the stinging crystals in the fruit, and secondly because of the tree's moderately short life. *INDOORS* Warmth and humidity are required for this fast-growing palm.

ARENGA UNDULATIFOLIA

A hugely broad, clumping palm. Very attractive, and requiring plenty of room to show it off adequately.

ORIGIN Borneo.

MATURE HEIGHT To 30ft, but usually much broader than tall.

TRUNK Multiple, messy, impenetrable, covered with old leaf fibers, usually hidden by the huge leaves.

LEAF Very long and wide pinnate leaf, it is similar to *A. pinnata*, but its distinctive and attractive wavy edges are unmistakable.

FLOWER STALK Growing among the leaves, as the other *Arenga* species.

FRUIT Round, a dark purplish red when ripe – handle with care!

SEED Usually three per fruit, with round backs and flattened faces to fit together.

CULTIVATION The seeds germinate quickly and easily if fresh. *OUTDOORS* This is a beautiful and fast-growing palm for the tropics. *INDOORS* Not much is known about its requirements inside, but these are likely to be satisfied by high humidity and warmth.

BACTRIS GASIPAES
PEACH PALM

A very spiny palm, this is grown commercially for its sweet fruit, often to be seen in the markets of its native countries.

ORIGIN Central and South America.

MATURE HEIGHT To 30ft.

TRUNK Clustering, slim, densely covered in black spines.

LEAF Pinnate, mid-green, with very spiny leafstalks.

FLOWER STALK From among the leaves.

FRUIT Yellow, the size and shape of a peach, grown as food in tropical countries.

SEED Round, ¾in in diameter, and very hard; sometimes missing from cultivated plants.

CULTIVATION Eating the fruit and planting the seed is twice the fun, and the latter germinate quite quickly. *OUTDOORS* Tropical conditions are required, with an abundance of water. Plants are quite fast-growing in favourable conditions. *INDOORS* This species is not known to have been tried indoors.

BISMARCKIA NOBILIS
BISMARCK PALM

A huge and attractive tropical fan palm, it is one of many unusual species which come from this interesting island.
ORIGIN Madagascar.
MATURE HEIGHT To 150 or 200ft.
TRUNK Stout, gray, smooth.
LEAF Huge fan leaf, up to 10ft across, blue gray in color.
FLOWER STALK From among the leaves.
FRUIT Round, 1½in in diameter.
SEED The size and shape of a walnut.
CULTIVATION The seeds germinate without any problems, usually within two to three months of sowing. The first leaves already have the distinctive color of the older tree. *OUTDOORS* A beautiful palm for the drier tropics. *INDOORS* Nothing is known of its cultural requirements indoors.

BORASSODENDRON MACHADONIS

This large fan palm makes an attractive plant for the tropical garden.
ORIGIN Malaysia, where it is rare.
MATURE HEIGHT To 100ft or more.
TRUNK Stout, gray, covered in closely arranged old leaf scars.
LEAF Fan-shaped, with characteristic deep splits between the broad segments.
FLOWER STALK From among the leaves.
FRUIT Large, round, 4 or 5in in diameter, glossy dark red brown.
SEED Usually 2 per fruit, 3in long, round on one side, flat on the other, covered in persistent, straw-colored, parallel fibers.
CULTIVATION The large seeds either germinate very quickly, or not at all; freshness would probably be the determining factor. *OUTDOORS* Tropical or subtropical conditions are required, together with a good water supply. *INDOORS* This has not been tried as a house plant.

BORASSUS FLABELLIFER

After the coconut, this is arguably the most numerous and widespread
palm in the world, and in its native India and Malaysia there are huge
stands covering thousands of acres. A sugary sap is obtained by cutting off
the unopened inflorescence, up to a gallon of sap being collected in this
way in a single day. It is a labor-intensive process; the natives climb up
each tree in turn, by means of a strap around their waist and the trunk, and
using the old leaf bases as footholds. The sap is then reduced, either by
boiling, to form a crude sugar, or by fermenting, to produce "toddy,"
which is an alcoholic liquor.

As well as this, the tree has literally hundreds of other uses. The timber is
very hard and black, and is much used in construction. The big leaves are
used in thatching and for paper, and the first long taproot produced by
the seed is a much sought-after vegetable delicacy.

BORASSUS FLABELLIFER
PALMYRA PALM

Very widely grown in the tropics, it is perhaps the most
numerous palm in the world.

ORIGIN India and Malaysia.

MATURE HEIGHT To 120ft.

TRUNK Thick, very hard, black and smooth.

LEAF Palmate, to 10ft across, forming a distinctive
spherical crown.

FLOWER STALK From among the leaves.

FRUIT Very large, to 6in in diameter, shiny dark brown in color.

SEED One to three per fruit. Large, covered in light brown,
wavy fibers like coarse fur.

CULTIVATION The seed produces a taproot 2 or 3ft long
before any top growth appears, so it should be planted
either in a deep container, or in its permanent position in
the ground. *OUTDOORS* This large palm is suitable for the
dry tropics. *INDOORS* It is unsuitable for use indoors.

BRAHEA ARMATA
MEXICAN BLUE PALM

In moonlight, the blue leaves of this beautiful and cold-hardy palm look almost white.

ORIGIN Southern California.

MATURE HEIGHT To 40ft.

TRUNK Solitary, thick and gray, either with persistent dead leaves, or smooth and covered with old leaf scars.

LEAF Stiff, palmate, covered with a pale blue bloom; looks its best in hot, bright and dry conditions.

FLOWER STALK From among the leaves, and arching out far beyond them.

FRUIT ½in in diameter, brown.

SEED Round.

CULTIVATION Germination is erratic, the seeds sometimes sprouting in a few weeks, sometimes taking a year or more. *OUTDOORS* This palm will grow in climates ranging from subtropical to temperate. It requires full sun, well drained soil, and an adequate supply of water. Slow-growing, especially in cooler areas, it has the advantage of being somewhat frost-tolerant. *INDOORS* The Mexican blue palm is probably not suitable for indoor cultivation because of its high light requirements, but it would tolerate dry air well and is a wonderful plant for the greenhouse or conservatory.

BRAHEA EDULIS
GUADALOUPE PALM

An attractive and fast-growing fan palm for temperate to subtropical regions.

ORIGIN Guadaloupe Island, off the Mexican coast.

MATURE HEIGHT To 50ft.

TRUNK Stout; old leaves self-prune, leaving leaf scars.

LEAF Mid-green, palmate, stiffly held.

FLOWER STALK From among the leaves.

FRUIT Hanging down in bunches, the fruits are dark brown to black, 1in in diameter, with an edible, though thin, sweet pulp.

SEED ¾in in diameter.

CULTIVATION The round seeds germinate more easily than those of *B. armata,* but germination still tends to be erratic. *OUTDOORS* This will grow outdoors from the subtropics to temperate zones, where it will stand some frost. Faster-growing than *B. armata,* it requires full sun, well-drained, rich soil, and an abundance of water. *INDOORS* Its high light requirements make it generally unsuitable for a house plant, but if this need can be fulfilled it would be worth a try.

BUTIA CAPITATA
BUTIA PALM, JELLY PALM

A popular and attractive palm for a wide range of climates, it is sometimes grown for the edible fruit, from which jam or jelly is made. This is one of the few hardy feather palms.

ORIGIN Brazil.
MATURE HEIGHT To 25ft.
TRUNK Gray, stout and smooth, but with old leaf scars.
LEAF Unmistakable – pinnate, strongly recurved, blue green in color.
FLOWER STALK From among the lower leaves.
FRUIT 1 in long, oval, yellow to red, with a sweet pulp.
SEED ¾in long, oval with three germination pores at one end.
CULTIVATION Seeds are erratic to germinate, and can take from a few weeks to a year or more. *OUTDOORS* The jelly palm grows in a wide range of climates, from subtropics to temperate regions, where it can withstand severe frosts. It prefers full sun and a well-drained soil, with plenty of water. *INDOORS* Its light requirements are probably too high for indoor cultivation, but if you have a very light area it would be worth a try.

CARYOTA MITIS
FISHTAIL PALM

An interesting and easily cultivated palm, it is commonly grown in the tropics, and readily available as a house plant.

ORIGIN Southeast Asia.
MATURE HEIGHT To 25 or 30ft.
TRUNK Multiple, slender.
LEAF Bipinnate, leaflets triangular, with a ragged edge and a distinctive "fishtail" shape.
FLOWER STALK Flowers appear from the highest leaf axil first, then progressively downward; when the last one has flowered and fruited, that stem dies, to be replaced by others in the clump.
FRUIT Round, ¾in in diameter, dull red when ripe; contains stinging crystals in the pulp, and should be handled with care.
SEED Round or hemispherical, with folds or grooves; dull gray in color.
CULTIVATION The distinctive seeds germinate easily and quickly if fresh. *OUTDOORS* Easily grown in the tropics, it is slower in the subtropics, though it may also be tried in warm temperate areas. Rich soil and an abundance of water are appreciated. *INDOORS* A good indoor palm, it tolerates low to medium light, but prefers bright indirect light, and humidity. Yellowing of the leaves may be caused by lack of iron.

CALAMUS

The palm genus with the largest number of species is *Calamus*, which contains nearly 400 members. It has a wide distribution, ranging from Africa to India and much of Southeast Asia, right down to Australia. The slim and flexible trunks, which snake up into the tree tops, are the source of rattan, much used in the manufacture of cane furniture. Although proper management of the industry is now becoming more and more widespread, many species are still considered to be endangered because of over-exploitation. Some methods of collection are very wasteful: sometimes elephants are used to drag the long canes down from the treetops. If one should break, then perhaps hundreds of feet are left suspended, inaccessible, and wasted. The Australian common name, "Wait-a-while," derives from the fact that to escape from entanglement in a *Calamus* clump can be a slow, not to mention a painful, experience.

CALAMUS AUSTRALIS
LAWYER'S CANE

Lawyer's cane is one of a huge family (containing almost 400 species) of spiny, mainly climbing palms from the tropics. The cleaned trunks, known as "Rattan," are used extensively in the manufacture of furniture.

ORIGIN Northeastern Australia.

MATURE HEIGHT Climbs up into the treetops, using other vegetation as a support.

TRUNK Multiple, very slender, sinuous, and covered with sharp spines.

LEAF Pinnate, pretty, with many regular, narrow leaflets; the leafstalk is covered with backward-pointing spines or hooks to aid its climbing habit, and the leaf may bear a long extension (up to 10ft long), similarly armed.

FLOWER STALK Long, pendulous, spiny.

FRUIT Pea-sized, a pale whitish green, covered with scales.

SEED Small, irregularly shaped.

CULTIVATION The small seeds must be absolutely fresh if they are to germinate, which they will do in a few weeks. *OUTDOORS* This can be grown in a tropical garden, where it should prove an interesting addition. *INDOORS* Young plants are extremely pretty. They should tolerate low light, but would be more fussy about humidity.

CARYOTA NO

A stunningly beautiful fishtail palm, with an incredibly complex leaf structure, this is one of the larger caryotas.

ORIGIN Mountainous districts of Borneo and peninsular Malaysia.
MATURE HEIGHT To 70ft.
TRUNK Thick, to 2ft in diameter, somewhat swollen towards the middle; light gray in color, with old leaf scars every foot or so, indicating the speed at which it grows.
LEAF Bipinnate, huge, and held flat; wonderful when viewed from below, in silhouette, leaflets are triangular, with ragged edges.
FLOWER STALK From the highest leaf axil first, then progressively downward; when the last one has flowered and fruited, the tree dies.
FRUIT 1½in in diameter, almost black when ripe, with caustic crystals in the pulp.
SEED One or two seeds per fruit, consequently round or half round in shape.
CULTIVATION The seeds germinate easily and quickly, if fresh.
OUTDOORS This *Caryota* is subtropical to tropical in its requirements.
INDOORS A good indoor palm, it will tolerate low to medium light, but prefers bright indirect light, and humidity. Yellowing of the leaves may be caused by lack of iron.

CARYOTA OBTUSA
FISHTAIL PALM

The largest of the fishtail palms, it is an awesome sight.
ORIGIN Northern India, China.
MATURE HEIGHT To 80 or 90ft.
TRUNK Massive, light gray, with old leaf scars.
LEAF Huge, bipinnate and flatly held.
FLOWER STALK From the highest leaf axil first, then progressively downward; when the last one has flowered and fruited, the tree dies.
FRUIT 1½in in diameter, dull red when ripe.
SEED One to three per fruit, shaped accordingly.
CULTIVATION The seeds germinate without difficulty. *OUTDOORS* Suitable for the tropics, subtropics and warm temperate regions, this is a hungry and thirsty palm. *INDOORS* Little is known of its requirements indoors, but these are likely to be the same as for the other fishtail palms.

CARYOTA URENS
WINE OR JAGGERY PALM

Both an alcoholic liquor and sugar are made from the sap.
ORIGIN India, Burma, Sri Lanka.
MATURE HEIGHT To 60ft.
TRUNK Solitary, gray with old leaf scars as rings every 12in or so, one for every old leaf.
LEAF Not held flat, but tumbling, arching and pendulous, leaflets are the usual fishtail shape, but are generally of a darker color than those of other species.
FLOWER STALK From the highest leaf axil first, then progressively downward; when the last one has flowered and fruited, the tree dies.
FRUIT ¾in circumference, dark red when ripe.
SEED One or two per fruit, thus round or half round; as with other caryotas, the fruit contains caustic crystals.
CULTIVATION Fresh seeds germinate easily and within a few weeks. *OUTDOORS* The wine palm can be grown in zones ranging from tropical to warm temperate. Rich soil, and an abundance of both water and fertilizer are required for optimum growth. *INDOORS* A good indoor palm, it will tolerate low to medium light, but prefers bright indirect light, and humidity. Yellowing of the leaves may be caused by lack of iron.

CEROXYLON ALPINUM
(SYN. C. ANDICOLA)
ANDEAN WAX PALM

This beautiful palm comes from the high Andes mountains of South America. The genus contains some of the tallest known plants, and the wax from the trunks is used commercially.
ORIGIN Colombia.
MATURE HEIGHT To 100ft.
TRUNK Solitary, slim, gray, covered with a layer of wax.
LEAF Pinnate, green above, silvery white beneath.
FLOWER STALK From among the leaf bases.
FRUIT ¾in in diameter, orange red when ripe, with a rough surface.
SEED ½in in diameter, round and very hard.
CULTIVATION The seeds germinate readily if very fresh; they lose their viability very quickly. Young plants seem to rot away quite easily and should be sprayed with fungicide immediately on germination and perhaps weekly thereafter until established. *OUTDOORS* An exciting palm for temperate and warm temperate areas, it is not suitable for the tropics. Plants will take some frost. *INDOORS* Nothing is known of its requirements as an indoor plant.

CEROXYLON QUINDIUENSE
ANDEAN WAX PALM

Similar to *C. alpinum* in many respects, but grows at a higher elevation, and is taller.

ORIGIN Colombia.
MATURE HEIGHT To an incredible 200ft.
TRUNK Smooth, gray, covered with a thin coating of wax.
LEAF Pinnate, green above, yellowish gray beneath.
FLOWER STALK From among the leaf bases.
FRUIT ¾in in diameter, orange red when ripe, with a smooth surface.
SEED ½in in diameter and very hard.
CULTIVATION The seeds germinate readily if very fresh; they speedily lose their viability. Young plants seem prone to rot; they should be sprayed with fungicide immediately on germination, and regularly thereafter until well established. *OUTDOORS* An exciting palm for temperate and warm temperate areas, and tolerant of frost to some extent, it is not suitable for the tropics. *INDOORS* Nothing is known of its requirements as an indoor plant.

CHAMAEROPS HUMILIS
MEDITERRANEAN FAN PALM

An extremely variable palm, it is commonly grown for cooler regions.
ORIGIN Western Mediterranean countries.
MATURE HEIGHT Cultivated plants can grow to 20ft, wild specimens rarely more than 3 or 4ft.
TRUNK Clumping, multiple, about 4 or 5in in diameter, in cultivation often forming a large bush; trunks are covered with old leaf bases.
LEAF Fan shaped, green, 2 or 3ft in diameter, very stiff leaflets; petiole armed with sharp spines; sometimes silver or blue forms are seen.
FLOWER STALK From among leaves.
FRUIT Round to oval, red brown when ripe, and 1in long.
SEED Oval, fibrous, ¾in.
CULTIVATION The seeds germinate in about six weeks. *OUTDOORS* Suitable for most climatic zones, this hardy palm is very cold-tolerant, surviving temperatures perhaps as low as −14°F. *INDOORS* It requires bright light to succeed, and is therefore not entirely suitable as a house plant, but it is an excellent conservatory plant.

CHAMEADOREA ELEGANS

The humble parlor palm, one of the most popular house palms in the world, comes from the rainforests of Mexico. Because of its tolerance of poor light, dry air, drought, flood and general neglect, it makes a very easy house plant. Additionally, seeds are produced when the palm is just two or three years old; germination is fast and reliable, and subsequent seedling growth is also speedy. All these advantages make this species a very attractive commercial proposition; parlor palms are grown by the million in Europe and America for the house plant trade. It is perfectly possible for parlor palms to produce seed at home, but as the sexes are on separate plants, two or more plants are required, and an even greater number increases the chances of successful pollination. When the tiny yellow flowers open, use a soft paintbrush to transfer pollen from one plant to another. Do this several times a day while the flowers are open. If you have been successful in aiding Mother Nature, the seeds will begin to develop within a few weeks – green at first, then black when ripe. When the first seed falls, the rest can be removed, dried and cleaned, and then planted to begin the process again.

CHAMEADOREA ELEGANS
PARLOR PALM

One of a large genus of some 100 species, this is so well known that it hardly needs any description. Tolerant of low light, and general abuse. It is very easily grown.

ORIGIN Mexico.

MATURE HEIGHT To 6 or 7ft.

TRUNK Slim, solitary, dark green, distinctly ringed with old leaf scars.

LEAF Dark green, pinnate.

FLOWER STALK From the lowest leaf axils.

FRUIT Small, round, black when ripe.

SEED Small, round.

CULTIVATION The parlor palm is easily grown from fresh seed. *OUTDOORS* It grows best in a shady position, with access to a steady supply of water, and will succeed in climates ranging from tropical to temperate. *INDOORS* Excellent as a house plant, living for a good number of years, it will stand low to medium light, and some cold.

CHAMEADOREA ERUMPENS
BAMBOO PALM

A beautiful and robust-growing palm, it is ideal as a house plant, as it tolerates low light and some cold.

ORIGIN Mexico.

MATURE HEIGHT To 10ft.

TRUNK Slim, multiple, dark green with prominent rings, like bamboo.

LEAF Dark green, pinnate, with fairly broad leaflets.

FLOWER STALK From the lowest leaf axils.

FRUIT Orange in color, and pea-sized.

SEED Small, round.

CULTIVATION The small seeds germinate easily if fresh. *OUTDOORS* Bamboo palms grow best in shade, as sun may burn the leaves. They form an attractive clump in a number of years. *INDOORS* A wonderful house plant, it will tolerate low light and cool conditions, and is fast-growing.

CHAMEADOREA GEONOMAEFORMIS

A small palm, with beautiful large leaves, it is not commonly available, but is worth seeking out, either for the home or for a yard in a warm area.

ORIGIN Mexico, Honduras.

MATURE HEIGHT Grows slowly to only 3 or 4ft.

TRUNK Slim, solitary, dark green, with old leaf scars as rings.

LEAF Large, simple, split into two halves.

FLOWER STALK From the lowest leaf axils.

FRUIT Black when ripe.

SEED Small, round.

CULTIVATION Seeds should be fresh to germinate well. *OUTDOORS* Plant in the warm yard in a shady spot, out of direct sunlight, which can burn the leaves. *INDOORS* This is another excellent indoor palm for position offering low to medium light.

CHAMEADOREA KLOTZSCHIANA

This is unusual in its leaf arrangement, which is unique in the palm world.

ORIGIN Mexico.

MATURE HEIGHT To 6ft.

TRUNK Solitary, slim, mid-green, with rings left by old leaves.

LEAF Pinnate, with leaflets arranged in irregular groups along the leaf stem.

FLOWER STALK From the lowest leaf axils.

FRUIT Black when ripe.

SEED Small, round.

CULTIVATION Rarely available, the seeds germinate readily if fresh. *OUTDOORS* As with other *Chameadoreas,* choose a shady spot, ideally in the tropical or subtropical garden. *INDOORS* Not much is known of its requirements, but these are likely to be the same as for other members of the genus.

CHAMEADOREA METALLICA

The unique quality of this species lies in the coloration of the leaves, which have a metallic sheen.

ORIGIN Mexico.

MATURE HEIGHT To only 3 or 4ft.

TRUNK Slim and dark green in color, with old leaf rings.

LEAF Simple, divided only at the tip, can range from dark green to almost black in color, with a unique metallic sheen.

FLOWER STALK From the lowest leaf axils, orange in color.

FRUIT Black when ripe.

SEED Small, oval.

CULTIVATION Fresh seeds germinate readily. *OUTDOORS* Shade is required if the leaves are to be a good, dark color. *INDOORS* A perfect indoor palm, it is elegant and attractive, very tolerant of low light, and should be more widely used.

CHAMEADOREA STOLONIFERA

An excellent house plant, it is grown for its attractively bushy shape.
ORIGIN Mexico.
MATURE HEIGHT To 6ft.
TRUNK Multiple, very slender, mid-green, each with leaf scars from fallen leaves; the slim stems run along the ground before turning upwards.
LEAF Simple, divided at the tip, mid-green.
FLOWER STALK From the lowest leaf axils.
FRUIT Black when ripe, oval.
SEED Small, oval.
CULTIVATION As with the other members of the genus, the small seeds should be fresh to ensure successful germination. *OUTDOORS* This species will perhaps take more sun than the others, but it still prefers a shady location, in a frost-free garden. *INDOORS* A wonderful house plant, it will tolerate low to medium light.

CHUNIOPHOENIX HAINANENSIS

A beautiful but rare palm, it is related to rhapis.
ORIGIN Hainan Island, China.
MATURE HEIGHT To 20ft.
TRUNK Slim, multiple.
LEAF Much like a very large *Rhapis* leaf, but with no hastula, a feature which distinguishes it from almost every other palm.
FLOWER STALK From among the leaves.
FRUIT Round, bright red when ripe, 1in in diameter.
SEED Round.
CULTIVATION Fresh seeds germinate well, and quickly, and subsequent seedling growth is also quite fast. *OUTDOORS* A warm temperate climate preferred, with high rainfall – frost-tolerance is probably minimal. *INDOORS* It has not been used in this way, but should be a good house plant.

CHRYSALIDOCARPUS LUTESCENS
BUTTERFLY PALM; ARECA PALM; GOLDEN CANE PALM

This is probably the most widely sold palm in the world.
ORIGIN Madagascar.
MATURE HEIGHT To 30ft, but usually seen as a pot plant.
TRUNK Multiple, slim, ringed, sometimes branching just above ground level.
LEAF Yellow petiole if sun-grown, otherwise green; leaf elegant, pale green feather-shaped.
FLOWER STALK From below the crownshaft.
FRUIT ¾in, oval.
SEED Oval, beaked at one end, dark red or brown.
CULTIVATION The butterfly palm is easily grown in warm temperate to tropical climates, fresh seeds germinating easily and quickly.
OUTDOORS This fast-growing, clumping palm will take either full sun or partial shade, and requires good drainage with lots of water.
INDOORS Perhaps the most popular house palm, it should have bright, indirect light, and does not like the cold.

CHRYSALIDOCARPUS MADAGASCARIENSIS

An attractive relative of *C. lutescens,* it is rarely seen outside botanic gardens.
ORIGIN Madagascar.
MATURE HEIGHT To 20 or 30ft.
TRUNK Solitary or multiple, 6in or more in diameter, gray and closely ringed with old leaf scars.
LEAF Plumose (leaflets are on different planes).
FLOWER STALK From below the crownshaft.
FRUIT Similar to *C. lutescens,* but a little smaller.
SEED ½in, beaked.
CULTIVATION This palm is easily grown from fresh seed. *OUTDOORS* A warm temperate to tropical climate is required, with full sun and ample moisture. *INDOORS* Not much tried, it probably requires bright indirect light.

COCCOTHRINAX ARGENTEA
FLORIDA SILVER PALM

This is a palm of bright sunshine, and dry, alkaline soils.
ORIGIN Southern Florida.
MATURE HEIGHT To 20ft.
TRUNK Solitary, slim, covered with woven fibers.
LEAF A small palmate leaf with distinctive silver undersides.
FLOWER STALK From among leaves.
FRUIT Small, round, brown when ripe.
SEED Tiny, round, wrinkled.
CULTIVATION Seeds germinate within a few weeks or months, but subsequent seedling growth is desperately slow, with one or two grass-like leaves per year. *OUTDOORS* The Florida silver palm requires bright sunshine in a tropical situation; it is well suited to coastal areas. *INDOORS* Not much tried indoors, it would undoubtedly have high light requirements.

COCCOTHRINAX CRINITA

An attractive small palm, it is well-known for the long, pale brown, hair-like fibers that cover the trunk.
ORIGIN Cuba.
MATURE HEIGHT To 20ft, perhaps more.
TRUNK Unmistakable, being completely covered in thick, long hair.
LEAF Fan-shaped, regularly cut.
FLOWER STALK From among the leaves.
FRUIT Small and round.
SEED Tiny, round, wrinkled.
CULTIVATION See notes under *C. argentea*.

COCOS NUCIFERA

"Nucifera" means "nut bearing," and "Cocos" comes from the Portuguese word for monkey, an allusion to the three pores or eyes of a coconut which are said to resemble a monkey's face. One of the world's most useful plants, the coconut palm has hundreds of uses and is the staple diet of many people in the tropics. Apart from the obvious use of the flesh (or "endosperm") as food, the coconut milk with which the nut is filled provides a refreshing drink. However, the most important use of this intensively farmed tree is the dried flesh, or "copra," which is exported by the millions of tons, and is used in the production of commercial oils.

Wild palms do not produce coconuts until they are many years old, and are very tall, but thanks to science, cultivated forms are mature when only four or five years old, with just a few feet of trunk. The large nuts can thus easily be gathered. It is as a symbol of all things tropical that the coconut palm is best known, and pictures of it are used to promote everything from vacations to shampoo, and from sunbeds to convertibles.

COCOS NUCIFERA
COCONUT PALM

Probably the best known palm in the world, it is used in a thousand ways to represent the tropics, its elegant, often leaning trunks standing as a symbol of tropical vacations.
ORIGIN Not known for sure, but probably the Pacific basin.
MATURE HEIGHT To 100ft, cultivars much less.
TRUNK Characteristic, often leaning, slim, solitary, ringed.
LEAF Feather-shaped, regular, green yellow in color.
FLOWER STALK From among the lower leaves.
FRUIT Oval, large to very large; yellow or green at first, then dry and brown when ripe.
SEED The well-known coconut.
CULTIVATION The large seeds take several months to germinate, and must be planted with the husk entire.
OUTDOORS This is a palm for the humid tropics; various cultivars are available, some of which fruit in only a few years, and when comparatively small. *INDOORS* Although it is often sold as a house plant, its requirements of high humidity, high temperature and high light, make it quite unsuitable. Most plants sold as house plants die within a few weeks or months.

COPERNICIA BAILEYANA
BAILEY'S COPERNICIA PALM

One of a diverse group of 25 species from Cuba and South America, many of which are beautiful, and a few of which are stunning. Grown for the wax that covers the leaves of some species, they also make striking ornamental palms for the tropics and subtropics.

ORIGIN Cuba.
MATURE HEIGHT To 50ft.
TRUNK Solitary, thick, smooth.
LEAF Large, stiff fan-shaped leaves covered with a thin layer of wax.
FLOWER STALK From among the leaf bases.
FRUIT Oval, 1in long, brown when ripe.
SEED Small, round, with a few wrinkles.
CULTIVATION The small seeds germinate easily enough, although they may take a few months. However, subsequent seedling growth is very slow, and big trees are a great age. *OUTDOORS* Wonderful ornamental palms for the tropics and subtropics, they appreciate much water during dry spells. *INDOORS* This species is not known to have been tried indoors.

COPERNICIA MACROGLOSSA
CUBAN PETTICOAT PALM

An unmistakable palm, it has stiff erect leaves which, when dead, form a dense skirt.

ORIGIN Cuba.
MATURE HEIGHT To 15ft.
TRUNK Solitary, bearing the huge petticoat of dead leaves.
LEAF The large, fan-shaped leaf is deeply cut and stiff.
FLOWER STALK From among the leaf bases.
FRUIT Oval, ¾in long.
SEED Small, round and wrinkled.
CULTIVATION Although easily germinated from seed, growth is very slow. *OUTDOORS* This is a palm for the tropics or subtropics, in sunny well-drained position. *INDOORS* It is not thought to have been tried as a house plant.

CORYPHA ELATA

This is a massive tropical palm. The genus produces the largest
flowering structure in the plant kingdom, the huge inflorescence
containing millions of flowers.

ORIGIN India, Burma.

MATURE HEIGHT To 70 or 80ft.

TRUNK Solitary, about 18in in diameter, sometimes with a faint spiral
pattern left by old leaf scars.

LEAF Huge, fan-shaped costapalmate leaf, perhaps 10ft across, the
massive petiole being edged with teeth.

FLOWER STALK The largest inflorescence of any flowering plant, it
grows at the very top of the mature tree, and produces millions of
flowers; after fruiting, the tree dies.

FRUIT Round, 1in in diameter.

SEED Round, produced in huge numbers.

CULTIVATION This palm is only suitable for large tropical parks. The
big seeds germinate readily, if fresh. *OUTDOORS* These huge trees take
up a lot of room, but if space is not a problem, they are a wonderful
addition to the tropical park. *INDOORS* Their requirements indoors are
little known, but doubtless seedlings could be grown for a while, given
sufficient humidity, warmth and light.

CORYPHA UMBRACULIFERA
TALIPOT PALM

One of the most massive palms, it is a fantastic sight when in flower,
with its huge trunk, leaves and inflorescence.

ORIGIN Sri Lanka.

MATURE HEIGHT To 80ft or more.

TRUNK Solitary, 24in in diameter, usually covered in old leaf bases,
and these in turn with epiphytic plants; scars are noticeable where old
leaves have fallen.

LEAF Huge costapalmate fan leaf, perhaps 15ft across; the petiole
armed with teeth along its edge.

FLOWER STALK See notes under *C. elata*.

FRUIT Round, the size of a golf ball, falling in great numbers when ripe.

SEED Large, round.

CULTIVATION See notes under *C. elata*.

CYRTOSTACHYS RENDA
SEALING WAX PALM, RAJAH PALM

A most beautiful and colourful palm, it is quite common in the tropics.
C. lakka is now synonymous with this species.
ORIGIN Malaysia.
MATURE HEIGHT To 15ft.
TRUNK Multiple, slim, distinctly ringed, with brilliant scarlet crownshaft and petioles.
LEAF Feather-shaped and quite stiffly held; the red coloration extends along the leafstalk in an unmistakable way.
FLOWER STALK From below the crownshaft.
FRUIT Small, ¾in, black when ripe.
SEED ½in, oval.
CULTIVATION The small seeds germinate quickly if fresh, but otherwise they can take several months. Definitely tropical in its requirements, it is slow-growing, but worth the wait. *OUTDOORS* A wonderful palm for tropical locations, it can take either full sun or shade, and requires adequate water. *INDOORS* Although a tempting subject, it is almost impossible to grow as a house plant, because of its tropical requirements.

DAEMONOROPS ANGUSTIFOLIA

This climbing rattan palm is equipped with sharp hooks and spines, which enable it to struggle up through other foliage in the rainforest.
ORIGIN Malaysia.
MATURE HEIGHT Determined by the surrounding vegetation, but may be very great indeed.
TRUNK Very slim, and covered in sharp spines, the stems of *Daemonorops* are used, after cleaning and sorting, to make rattan furniture and other items.
LEAF Rather pretty and regular, feather-shaped leaf, with the central stem extending way beyond the leaf tip, and modified into a climbing aid (a "cirrus") with many backward-facing hooks, which should be treated with respect as they are quite dangerous.
FLOWER STALK Grows from between the leaf bases.
FRUIT Rather attractive, covered with overlapping scales, sometimes oozing a red liquid called "dragon's blood."
SEED Small, round.
CULTIVATION The small seeds germinate readily if fresh. *OUTDOORS* Care should be exercised because of its dangerous nature, but it is perfectly possible to grow this palm in the wet tropics. *INDOORS* Its regular leaflets would make it an attractive house plant, which could be grown for a few years. Humidity is essential.

DECKENIA NOBILIS
PALMISTE

A beautiful, tall palm from the Seychelles, it is rare in its natural habitat, and also in cultivation, though occasional specimens may be found in botanic gardens.
ORIGIN Seychelles Islands.
MATURE HEIGHT To 100ft.
TRUNK Slim, closely ringed, covered – when young – with sharp spines, a feature not seen on older trees.
LEAF Feather-shaped, their bases forming a crownshaft.
FLOWER STALK From below the crownshaft.
FRUIT ½in long, approximately heart-shaped; black when ripe.
SEED Roughly heart-shaped.
CULTIVATION Seeds germinate quickly and easily if very fresh. *OUTDOORS* This is well worth trying for its rarity alone, though tropical conditions are certainly required. *INDOORS* Nothing is known of its requirements as a house plant.

DICTYOSPERMA ALBUM
PRINCESS PALM; HURRICANE PALM

This is reasonably common in cultivation, small plants sometimes even being available in supermarkets, but it is very rare in the wild. A red form – *D. album* var. *rubrum* – is also seen.
ORIGIN Mascarene Islands.
MATURE HEIGHT To around 30ft.
TRUNK Distinctively swollen at the base, gray, solitary, often with vertical fissures; crownshaft.
LEAF Broad and feather-shaped.
FLOWER STALK From below the crownshaft.
FRUIT ¾in long, egg-shaped, dark red to black when ripe.
SEED Egg-shaped, pointed, with scar from one end to the other.
CULTIVATION The seeds germinate quickly and easily. *OUTDOORS* This palm makes a handsome addition to any tropical collection. *INDOORS* An attractive house plant, especially the red variety, it likes warmth and humidity, but not cold.

ELAEIS GUINEENSIS

Why is the oil palm so called? The answer is that one of the most important vegetable oils in the world is produced by this rather untidy palm. Originally from Africa, it is now widespread throughout the tropics and is grown by the million for this important crop. Sometimes you can drive for hours without seeing anything other than plantations of this tree.

The fruit, from which the oil comes, is produced when the tree is comparatively young, and genetic engineering has played its part in this acceleration of nature. The fruits are produced in large and heavy clusters, which are cut out of the crown of the tree with a special long-handled knife. Rats and snakes also live alongside the fruits, so this is not the most pleasant of jobs. The fruit clumps are then barrowed to the roadside to await collection by trucks.

At the factory, immensely strong crushing machines are used to extract the oil, which is then moved by tankers. It is a huge industry, worth millions of dollars annually, and is one of the biggest exports of many tropical countries.

ELAEIS GUINEENSIS
OIL PALM

Planted commercially by the million in tropical countries for the edible oil contained in the fruit and seeds, it is rapidly replacing the rainforests in Malaysia.
ORIGIN West Africa.
MATURE HEIGHT To 60 or 70ft, usually much less in cultivated specimens.
TRUNK To 18in thick, covered with untidy old leaf bases and often epiphytic plants and ferns.
LEAF Feather-shaped, the leaflets being in two planes, giving a slightly plumose appearance.
FLOWER STALK From among the leaf bases.
FRUIT In large, tight bunches, yellow, then red, and finally glossy black at maturity; an extremely important tropical crop in many countries, plantations covering hundreds of square miles.
SEED 1in, very hard, pointed at one end.
CULTIVATION The hard seeds germinate with some difficulty. *OUTDOORS* Not a very attractive palm, it must be said, it is, however, easily grown in the tropics. *INDOORS* The oil palm can be grown on for a few years as a young plant, requiring warmth and humidity for good results.

EUGEISSONA TRISTIS
BERTAM

Locally a very common palm, it is unusual outside its native habitat, and is not often seen even in botanic gardens. It is a forest pest in some areas, where it forms great colonies to the exclusion of all other plants.
ORIGIN Malaysia.
MATURE HEIGHT To 25ft.
TRUNK None, the leaves rising directly from the underground stem; these palms form large, untidy clumps.
LEAF To 25ft long, feather-shaped, stalks spiny.
FLOWER STALK Curious woody flower stalk rising erect from among the leaves.
FRUIT Large, 2in long by 1in, oval, pointed at both ends, covered with tiny scales.
SEED Oval, with deep ridges and grooves along its length.
CULTIVATION The large seeds germinate in eight to ten weeks. *OUTDOORS* A tropical climate with seasonally dry conditions is best for this palm. *INDOORS* Nothing is known of its indoor requirements.

EUTERPE EDULIS
ASSAI PALM

An important crop-palm in South America, where it is grown for "heart of palm" or "palmito." This attractive small palm is sometimes sold as a house plant.
ORIGIN Brazil.
MATURE HEIGHT To 80ft.
TRUNK Slim and attractive, with a prominent green crownshaft.
LEAF Elegant, feather leaf, with many narrow leaflets.
FLOWER STALK From below crownshaft.
FRUIT Round, ½in, almost black when ripe.
SEED Round.
CULTIVATION Fresh seeds germinate readily. *OUTDOORS* The Assai palm prefers tropical conditions, although there is some evidence that this species can grow well in cooler climates. *INDOORS* An excellent house plant, it is tolerant of low light and is easily cared for. It is usual, and best, to plant several to a pot.

GASTROCOCOS CRISPA
CUBAN BELLY PALM

This striking and unusual palm has a swollen trunk, which gives it its common name.

ORIGIN Cuba.

MATURE HEIGHT To 45ft.

TRUNK Solitary, smooth and ringed, swollen about or above the middle, and very spiny.

LEAF Feather, dark green above, paler beneath, with a spiny petiole.

FLOWER STALK From among the leaves.

FRUIT 1in in diameter.

SEED Small, round.

CULTIVATION The small seeds are erratic to germinate, but subsequent growth is reasonably fast. *OUTDOORS* Tropical to subtropical climates, and full sun, would suit this handsome palm best. *INDOORS* It is not known to have been tried as a house plant.

GUIHAYAIA ARGYRATA

Pronounced "Gwee-higher," this is a recently described, attractive palm from southern China, where it grows in tiny crevices, often on sheer rock faces. Perhaps it is totally non-competitive and these are thus the only sites available to it. It is hoped that this attractive palm will become more common as its potential is explored.

ORIGIN South China, quite common in the Guilin area.

MATURE HEIGHT A few feet.

TRUNK The plant is usually stunted by the situation of its growth, and thus trunkless, in better conditions a small trunk may emerge.

LEAF Unique among palms, it is fan shaped, with reduplicate (roof- as opposed to valley-shaped) leaflets; it also has a brilliant white-silvery back to the leaf, unsuspected when seen from above.

FLOWER STALK From among the leaf bases.

FRUIT Small, round, black when ripe.

SEED Small, round.

CULTIVATION The small seeds germinate erratically. *OUTDOORS* It would presumably require dry conditions, and certainly full sun. Very slow-growing in its natural habitat, it is probably faster in cultivation, and could be grown in a tropical, subtropical, or warm temperate climate. *INDOORS* Well worth trying if and when available, bright light, and drying-out between waterings are probably essential.

HEDESCEPE CANTERBURYANA
UMBRELLA PALM

This grows on exposed and windswept ridges of its island home, and is thus ideal for planting in coastal areas.

ORIGIN Lord Howe Island, a tiny dot in the ocean off the east coast of Australia; this is also the home of the howeas.

MATURE HEIGHT To 25ft.

TRUNK Solitary, gray, with crownshaft.

LEAF Not unlike the kentia palm leaf, being feather-shaped, coarse, and dark green.

FLOWER STALK From below the crownshaft.

FRUIT Large, up to 2in long, oval, and dark red when ripe.

SEED Large, slightly longer than wide, with a characteristic broad scar down one side.

CULTIVATION Seeds are difficult and erratic to germinate. *OUTDOORS* Good for exposed position, it is slow-growing, but will tolerate high winds and salt spray. *INDOORS* An excellent indoor palm, it is tolerant of low light and slow-growing.

HOWEA BELMOREANA
SENTRY PALM

This is well known, mainly because of its more famous brother, the kentia palm, *H. forsteriana,* to which it is similar in many respects.

ORIGIN Lord Howe Island, off eastern Australia.

MATURE HEIGHT To 25ft.

TRUNK Slim, dark green in young plants, gray in older trees, ringed with old leaf scars; no crownshaft.

LEAF Dark green, leathery texture, feather-shaped, with the leaflets pointing upwards forming a "V" shape.

FLOWER STALK A single spike, pendulous, from below lowest leaves; the stalks of several seasons may be on the tree at the same time, the pollen from one fertilizing the flowers on the previous season's flower stalk below.

FRUIT The size and shape of an olive, but sharper at each end; takes two years to ripen, at which time it turns from green to dark brown.

SEED Oval.

CULTIVATION The seeds are slow and erratic to germinate, and it is essential that they are fresh. *OUTDOORS* It is a palm for temperate and warm temperate areas and will not do well in the tropics, seeming to enjoy fresh air and breezy conditions. It must have shade when young, but will later tolerate full sun. *INDOORS* Not as popular as its relative, it is still very useful indoors, where it tolerates low light and neglect.

HOWEA FORSTERIANA
KENTIA PALM

One of the most popular and indeed most suitable palms in the world for interior use, it was introduced into Europe during Victorian times, and has been popular ever since. It was used by the Victorians to good effect for their "Palm Court orchestras."

ORIGIN Lord Howe Island, off the east coast of Australia.

MATURE HEIGHT To 50ft.

TRUNK Slim, dark green with prominent rings when young, gray and less prominently ringed when older.

LEAF Broad, dark green, feather-shaped, leathery texture, leaflets held in a flat plane and not rising upwards, like those of *H. belmoreana*.

FLOWER STALK From below the lowest leaves, multiple; several seasons' stalks may be on the trunk at any one time, pollen from one falling to fertilize the last season's flowers below.

FRUIT Bigger than *H. belmoreana*, but similar in shape; dark brown when ripe, which can take two years.

SEED Oval, a little larger than those of *H. belmoreana*.

CULTIVATION Seeds are again erratic and difficult to germinate, and should be absolutely fresh for best results. *OUTDOORS* It requires a sunny position in temperate or warm temperate areas, and shade when young. *INDOORS* Unsurpassed as an indoor subject, it will tolerate low light and general abuse.

HYDRIASTELE
MICROSPADIX

A pretty, slim, clump-forming, tropical palm, with distinctive arrangements of leaflets, it is worthy of greater use.

ORIGIN New Guinea.

MATURE HEIGHT To 40ft.

TRUNK Several, slim, forming an attractive clump; crownshaft.

LEAF Feather-shaped, with an irregular arrangement of both narrow and broad leaflets with squared-off ends, most noticeable in silhouette.

FLOWER STALK From below the crownshafts.

FRUIT Small, round, bright red when ripe.

SEED Small, ½in round, covered with fibers.

CULTIVATION The small seeds germinate easily, but may take some months to do so and must be fresh. *OUTDOORS* A useful, small clumping palm for the moist tropics. *INDOORS* It is not known to be used in the home.

HYOPHORBE LAGENICAULIS
BOTTLE PALM

This unusual palm is well named, as its trunk really is the shape of a bottle. It is virtually extinct in the wild.

ORIGIN Mascarene Islands.

MATURE HEIGHT To only about 10ft.

TRUNK The great bulging trunk, sometimes regular with visible rings, sometimes irregular with less noticeable rings, is one of the curiosities of the plant kingdom. This tapers to the point where it forms a crownshaft, itself usually swollen for the first few inches.

LEAF Very stiff, feather-shaped, often twisted and recurved; there are only four or five leaves, even on a mature tree.

FLOWER STALK From below the crownshaft.

FRUIT Oval, 1½in by 1in.

SEED Oval in shape, with raised "veins" on the surface.

CULTIVATION The seeds germinate easily if fresh, though the process may take some weeks, or months. *OUTDOORS* A wonderful subject for tropical locations, it will tolerate full sun and salt spray, and requires plenty of water. *INDOORS* It is not much used in interiors, although it is very suitable if conditions are warm enough, and there is sufficient light.

HYOPHORBE VERSCHAFFELTII
SPINDLE PALM

A close relative of *H. lagenicaulis,* it is distinguished by the different shape of its trunk. A very attractive palm, and planted widely in the tropics, it is occasionally used in interiors, where it commands much attention.

ORIGIN Mascarene Islands, where it is almost extinct in the wild state.

MATURE HEIGHT To 20ft.

TRUNK Spindle-shaped (narrow at the base), becoming wider half way up, and then tapering again to the swollen crown shaft; rings or scars left by old leaves.

LEAF Quite stiff, more erect and less recurved than the bottle palm, otherwise similar.

FLOWER STALK From below the swollen crownshaft.

FRUIT 1in, oval.

SEED Long and narrow.

CULTIVATION The seeds may take several weeks or months to germinate, and care should be taken that they are fresh. *OUTDOORS* A showy and unusual palm for tropical locations, it needs full sun and sufficient moisture. *INDOORS* This is a good palm for indoor use, but requires warmth and good light.

HYPHAENE DICHOTOMA
DOUM PALM

One of the few truly branching palms, and regarded as a curiosity because of it. In its own way, this unmistakable palm is a beautiful tree, but only rarely seen. A palm of the dry and arid plains and semi-deserts.
ORIGIN East coast of India.
MATURE HEIGHT To 60ft.
TRUNK Slender but much branched, each branch dividing again and again, and ending in a crown of leaves.
LEAF Heavily costapalmate, that is, the petiole extending into the leaf blade and giving a twisted appearance; the leaf itself is hard, waxy and durable.
FLOWER STALK From among the leaf bases.
FRUIT The shape and size of a pear, very hard, and an orange-brown color.
SEED Extremely difficult to extract from the fruit, being very hard and bony.
CULTIVATION The large seeds can germinate extremely quickly, or can sometimes take many weeks. They require a deep pot, as the first root grows very long as it seeks out ground moisture. *OUTDOORS* An unusual, slow-growing ornamental for hot and dry areas, it will also grow in the humid tropics. *INDOORS* Nothing is known of its indoor requirements, but its need for bright light would be a limiting factor.

JOHANNESTEJSMANNIA ALTIFRONS

A wonderful and fabulous tropical palm, its huge undivided leaves are much prized as thatching in its native land.
ORIGIN Malaysia.
MATURE HEIGHT To about 10ft.
TRUNK None, the leaves rising direct from an underground stem.
LEAF Huge, simple, to 6 or 7ft long and 2 or 3ft wide.
FLOWER STALK From among the leaf bases.
FRUIT Round, about 1in, with a warty, corky surface.
SEED Round and slightly flattened.
CULTIVATION This exciting palm is becoming more common in botanical collections, and deserves to be more widely grown. The seeds must be fresh and are erratic to germinate. *OUTDOORS* Requiring a shaded position in the moist tropics, it is slow-growing, but well worth the wait. It is essential to afford protection from wind, which would easily damage the huge leaves. *INDOORS* Plants would probably only survive in a hot and moist greenhouse, which closely imitates the tropical conditions they require.

JUBAEA CHILENSIS

This huge palm tree (it has the thickest trunk of any palm), once common in its native Chile, has been over-exploited in the past for the manufacture of "palm wine." A mature trunk can contain up to 100 gallons of sugary sap, which is boiled down to make palm honey, or fermented to produce the alcoholic liquor. The collection of this sap results in the death of the tree, and it is now rare in some areas where it was once the main component of the vegetation.

Fortunately, it is now a protected tree in its native country, and it is also being extensively replanted for the production of the nuts, called "coquitos" (little coconuts), which are both edible and delicious, tasting just like real coconuts (*Cocos nucifera*).

JUBAEA CHILENSIS
CHILEAN WINE PALM

A palm of awesome size — unmistakable with its massive trunk — it is much planted in botanic gardens and public parks in most of the warm temperate parts of the world. In its native Chile, a wine is made from the sap.

ORIGIN Chile, where it is now endangered, due to excessive felling.

MATURE HEIGHT To 70ft.

TRUNK Massive, to 5 or 6ft in diameter, gray, smooth, with faint flattened diamond-shaped old leaf scars; no crownshaft.

LEAF Feather, coarse, leathery texture, leaflets reduplicate (roof- as opposed to valley-shaped).

FLOWER STALK From among the leaves.

FRUIT Round, 1½in in diameter, yellow.

SEED 1in in circumference, hard and bony, with an edible flesh, tasting like coconut.

CULTIVATION If fresh, the large seeds germinate without additional heat in a few months. *OUTDOORS* Not happy in the tropics, this is an essential palm for all warm temperate regions, and will tolerate severe cold and frost once established. As it is very slow-growing, it is usually future generations that benefit from the planting of this wonderful palm. *INDOORS* It can be grown indoors, but needs bright, indirect light, and is extremely slow-growing.

JUBAEAOPSIS CAFFRA
PONDOLAND PALM

This rarely encountered palm is now creating more attention, and is occasionally seen in collections. It is related to the *Jubaea* genus.
ORIGIN Northeastern South Africa, restricted to only a few sites, where it grows on river banks.
MATURE HEIGHT To 20ft.
TRUNK Multiple, slim, covered with old leaf scars.
LEAF Feather, coarse-textured and leathery.
FLOWER STALKS From among the leaves.
FRUIT Like *Jubaea* in many respects.
SEED Very similar to *Jubaea.*
CULTIVATION This has not been much tried, firstly because seeds are difficult to obtain (many trees overhang the water and the seeds are lost), and secondly because they are extremely difficult to germinate. *OUTDOORS* The Pondoland palm would require a warm and sunny position, with adequate water. *INDOORS* It is not known to have been tried indoors.

LACCOSPADIX AUSTRALASICA
ATHERTON PALM

An Australian palm, rapidly gaining popularity in that country as a house plant, it will undoubtedly become more available in future years, but at present is rare outside of its native home.
ORIGIN Northeast Australia, in rainforests.
MATURE HEIGHT To 10ft.
TRUNK Slim, solitary or multiple, dark green, ringed.
LEAF Feather, delicate in appearance.
FLOWER STALK From among the leaf bases.
FRUIT Very pretty, hanging on pendulous single spikes, bright red when ripe.
SEED Small, round.
CULTIVATION This is excellent either for indoors or outdoors (in temperate to tropical zones). The small seeds may be erratic in germination and the young plants grow slowly. It is not thought to be frost-hardy. *OUTDOORS* A moist, shady area in the garden, with a steady supply of water at all times, would suit this attractive small palm. *INDOORS* A wonderful indoor palm, it will tolerate much-reduced light levels and should be treated in the same way as a *Chameadorea.*

LATANIA LODDIGESSII
BLUE LATAN PALM

Three beautiful and distinct stiff-leaved fan palms form the *Latania* genus. Though common in cultivation, they are thought to be almost extinct in their native home.

ORIGIN Mascarene Islands.

MATURE HEIGHT To 40ft.

TRUNK Slim, gray, ringed indistinctly with scars of old leaves.

LEAF Very stiff, fan-shaped, glaucous blue green in color, costapalmate (the leaf stalk extends well into the leaf); the bases divide into two where they join the trunk.

FLOWER STALK From among the leaf bases.

FRUIT Large and plum-like, dark brown when ripe, usually containing three seeds per fruit.

SEED Interestingly sculpted, broader at one end, and looking as though carved; a prominent ridge runs along the length.

CULTIVATION Plants are easily grown from seed, which germinates in a few weeks if fresh. *OUTDOORS* A sunny position in tropics or subtropics is required, together with adequate water in dry weather, and a well-drained soil. Plants can be quite fast-growing. *INDOORS* This shows some promise as an interior plant, but it requires good bright light, and benefits from humidity, though the latter appears not to be essential.

LATANIA LONTAROIDES
RED LATAN PALM

The young plants have a beautiful red coloration on the leaves and leaf stalks. An attractive and strong-growing palm, it is not uncommon in cultivation.

ORIGIN Reunion Island, where it is almost extinct.

MATURE HEIGHT To 40ft.

TRUNK Slim, solitary, gray, about 8in in diameter.

LEAF Stiff fan-shaped, costapalmate leaves, with red-purple coloration, especially in juvenile plants.

FLOWER STALK From among the leaf bases.

FRUIT Large and plum-like, dark brown when ripe.

SEED Round at one end, pointed at the other; "sculpturing" much less apparent than with the other two species.

CULTIVATION The seeds germinate easily if fresh, but may take several weeks. *OUTDOORS* This is another wonderful palm for the tropical or subtropical garden; sun, good drainage and adequate watering in dry weather will promote good growth. *INDOORS* While it is not known to be used as a house plant, it would be well worth a try. Bright light would certainly be required.

LATANIA VERSCHAFFELTII
YELLOW LATAN PALM

Its quite striking yellow coloration easily identifies this attractive, tropical palm.

ORIGIN Rodrigues Island in the Indian Ocean, where it is now extremely rare.

MATURE HEIGHT To 40ft.

TRUNK Slim, gray, solitary, old leaf scars leaving rings.

LEAF Hard and durable, strong yellow or golden coloration of the leaf stalk, and veins, especially noticeable in younger plants; costapalmate.

FLOWER STALK From among the leaf bases.

FRUIT Large, the shape and size of a plum, brown when ripe.

SEED Looking as though sculptured, or moulded, with ridges in a quite intricate pattern, beaked at one end.

CULTIVATION Easily cultivated from seed, which germinates in a few weeks or months. *OUTDOORS* A sunny position in the tropical or subtropical garden would suit this palm best, and although they show some resistance to drought, adequate watering during dry weather would be beneficial. *INDOORS* Not thought to be grown indoors, it would perhaps do well, given enough light and warmth.

LICUALA GRANDIS
RUFFLED FAN PALM

Immediately recognizable for its beautiful leaves, *Licuala grandis* is but one in a genus of over 100 species. Essentially a tropical palm, it is occasionally sold as a house plant.

ORIGIN New Hebrides, a group of islands off the north coast of Australia.

MATURE HEIGHT To 8 or 9ft.

TRUNK Slim, solitary, a few inches only in diameter, gray.

LEAF Unmistakable: a beautiful, circular, undivided and regularly pleated leaf, about 24in in diameter or more, with a notched edge.

FLOWER STALK From among the leaf bases.

FRUIT Bright red when ripe, small and round.

SEED Small, round, with a segmented appearance, like a peeled orange.

CULTIVATION Essentially a tropical palm, its small seeds germinate in a few weeks – without difficulty, if fresh. *OUTDOORS* A sunny or shaded position in a humid, tropical location is the ideal spot for this small palm tree. *INDOORS* It may certainly be grown indoors, but steps must be taken to ensure adequate humidity, and warmth. Air that is too dry invariably results in the edges of the leaves browning. The best places in the home are probably the bathroom or kitchen.

LICUALA ORBICULARIS

Perhaps the most beautiful of the *Licualas*, and thus of the palms, its leaf has to be seen to be believed. One unfortunate local use is as a temporary umbrella – it is heartbreaking to see leaves discarded after a brief shower.

ORIGIN Borneo.

MATURE HEIGHT To 10ft perhaps.

TRUNK None, the leaf stalks rising direct from the underground rootstock.

LEAF Circular and glossy, to 3 or 4ft in diameter, and held flat, unlike *L. grandis*, which is undulating – fabulous!

FLOWER STALK From among the leaf bases.

FRUIT Round, $\frac{1}{2}$in in diameter, red when ripe.

SEED Small, round.

CULTIVATION The seeds, which are slowly becoming more available, germinate in a few weeks or months. Subsequent seedling growth is slow. *OUTDOORS* Shelter from wind is the most important condition for this beautiful palm. The slightest breeze will ruin the huge leaves. It is absolutely tropical in its other requirements. *INDOORS* It's tempting to try this palm as an interior subject, but do so only if you can provide year-round warmth and high humidity, for instance in a tropical glasshouse. Low to medium light is preferred.

LICUALA SPINOSA

Its relationship to *L. grandis* is easily seen; its leaf looks much like a split-up ruffled fan leaf, and it is perhaps the best *licuala* for interior use.

ORIGIN From southern Thailand, down through Malaysia, to western Indonesia.

MATURE HEIGHT To 12 or 13ft.

TRUNK Multiple, slim, clustering, ending up as a dense bush.

LEAF Circular in shape, but divided to the base into irregular leaflets, with squared-off ends; the very first seedling leaf also has a squared tip.

FLOWER STALK From among the leaf bases.

FRUIT Round, the size of a marble, red when ripe.

SEED Small and round.

CULTIVATION If fresh, the seeds will germinate within a few weeks or months. *OUTDOORS* Though again a tropical species, *L. spinosa* wil also succeed in the sub-tropics. *INDOORS* This is perhaps the most successful of the *licualas* for use indoors, where it seems slightly less fussy about humidity. Also, the leaves are thicker and more leathery and thus resist dry air better. Medium to low light is tolerated well.

LIVISTONA AUSTRALIS
AUSTRALIAN FAN PALM

This is one of a genus containing some 30 species, distributed from the Middle East through Southeast Asia to Australia. Many are cultivated as ornamental plants, from temperate to tropical zones.
ORIGIN Eastern Australia – it is thus one of the most southerly growing palms in the world.
MATURE HEIGHT To 50ft.
TRUNK Solitary, gray, about 12in in diameter.
LEAF Fan-shaped, with distinctively drooping tips; the petiole (leaf stalk) is edged with very sharp teeth.
FLOWER STALK From among the leaves.
FRUIT Round, ¾in in diameter, red brown when ripe.
SEED Round, ½in in diameter.
CULTIVATION The seeds germinate quickly and easily, and subsequent seedling growth is quite fast. *OUTDOORS* Growing in climates from temperate to tropical, it prefers full sun but can do well in shade and well-drained soil, with an adequate supply of water in dry weather. *INDOORS* It is perfectly possible to grow this palm indoors, but it requires bright, indirect light.

LIVISTONA CHINENSIS
CHINESE FAN PALM, FOUNTAIN PALM

This is a popular species, both as an indoor and an outdoor specimen.
ORIGIN Southern China.
MATURE HEIGHT To 40ft.
TRUNK Solitary, some 12in in diameter, often enlarged at the base; gray in color, with barely distinguishable rings.
LEAF Fan-shaped, longer than wide, with a spiny petiole, and strongly drooping leaf tips, earning it the common name of fountain palm.
FLOWER STALK From among the leaf bases.
FRUIT Oval, dark green in color, 1in in length.
SEED Oval, pale brown in color, ¾in long.
CULTIVATION The fountain palm is easily cultivated from seed, which germinates readily and quickly. *OUTDOORS* It is a popular palm in all areas, from temperate to tropical; full sun, and adequate water in dry weather will ensure success. *INDOORS* Equally popular as a house plant, it requires bright, indirect light.

LIVISTONA ROTUNDIFOLIA
FOOTSTOOL PALM

A distinctive *livistona*, somewhat more tropical in its requirements than the others, it is generally more tidy in appearance.

ORIGIN Malaysia, Indonesia, Philippines.

MATURE HEIGHT To 50ft.

TRUNK Slim, pale gray, some forms having a distinctively ringed trunk, though this is uncommon; only some 8in in diameter.

LEAF Fan-shaped, round and very regular in appearance, often forming a deep crown, much taller than wide.

FLOWER STALK From among the leaf bases.

FRUIT ¾in round, and red brown when ripe.

SEED ½in in circumference, pale brown.

CULTIVATION The seeds germinate easily and quickly. *OUTDOORS* This is a beautiful fan palm for the tropics, especially the more unusual forms, which are worth seeking out. *INDOORS* The young plants are very attractive, with their regular, shallowly divided leaves, their main requirements being bright, indirect light, and an adequate supply of water.

LODOICEA MALDIVICA
COCO-DE-MER, DOUBLE COCONUT

This fabulous palm bears the largest seed in the vegetable kingdom, a single one weighing up to 40lb.

ORIGIN Unique to the Seychelles Islands in the Indian Ocean.

MATURE HEIGHT To 80ft.

TRUNK Solitary, very tall, but not especially thick.

LEAF Very large, fan-shaped, strongly costapalmate; in the valleys where they grow, the huge leaves crash into one another during gales, making an awesome noise.

FLOWER STALK From among the leaf bases.

FRUIT Very large, up to 15in long, taking five years to ripen.

SEED Looking like a 2-lobed coconut, the largest seed in the world, and the heaviest.

CULTIVATION Seeds are difficult to obtain, and expensive. They need to be planted in their permanent position as they produce a long taproot. Alternatively, they can be started off in a large pot. They may take over a year to germinate. *OUTDOORS* This is a palm for the humid tropics, but even in this region they are considered difficult to establish. *INDOORS* Attempts have been made to grow them in tropical greenhouses, with some success. Even the very first leaf is huge, and much space is therefore required.

LYTOCARYUM WEDDELLIANUM
MINIATURE COCONUT PALM

Formerly listed as *Microcoeleum Weddellianum*, this is a graceful and dainty palm, most often seen as a small pot plant, and as such they are sold by the thousand in plant centers and supermarkets.

ORIGIN Brazil.

MATURE HEIGHT Only to about 6ft.

TRUNK Only about 2in thick, often much less, and ringed.

LEAF Very fine and delicate feather leaf, with fine leaflets a glossy green in colour.

FLOWER STALK From among the leaf bases.

FRUIT ¾in in circumference, looking like a tiny coconut.

SEED ½in in diameter, with three pores, or "eyes."

CULTIVATION The small seeds germinate within a few weeks. *OUTDOORS* A shady position in the subtropical garden would be ideal. Humidity is appreciated and keeps the plant looking fresh. Although slow-growing, it is well worth the wait, as it is surely one of the most beautiful of the small palms. It will also grow in cooler, but frost-free, areas. Shade is essential, and the extremely fragile roots make it almost impossible to transplant. *INDOORS* A popular house plant, it is usually grown commercially in clay pots without drainage holes to avoid the necessity of cutting the roots, which would mean the death of the plant. It is tolerant of low light, and appreciative of humidity.

METROXYLON SAGU
SAGO PALM

Easily recognizable for its erect habit, and its fruits, it is an important source of sago in its native home, and often seen around villages in the tropics. The trunks are felled as they are about to flower, and the sago is extracted from the split trunk.

ORIGIN Southeast Asia.

MATURE HEIGHT To 30ft.

TRUNK Clump-forming, with one or two main stems; each trunk dies after fruiting, to be replaced by others.

LEAF Feather-shaped, held stiffly upright, curving gently out towards the top, which gives the species a distinctive silhouette.

FLOWER STALK Produced terminally from the top of the trunk, in the manner of the *Corypha* genus.

FRUIT The size of a golf ball, pear-shaped, covered with attractive overlapping scales, like the skin of a reptile.

SEED 1½in in circumference, with one side concave.

CULTIVATION The seeds are difficult and erratic to germinate, and may take some months to do so. *OUTDOORS* This is very much a palm for the tropics, where it is happy in moist (even swampy) ground in full sun. The fact that it is fast-growing, and that it dies after fruiting, may be a disadvantage for the gardener. *INDOORS* Nothing is known of its indoor requirements.

NANNORRHOPS RITCHIANA
MAZARI PALM

This is a mystery palm, in so far as it is extremely common in its native homelands, but extremely rare in cultivation, and is only now slowly finding its way on to specialists' lists. There are only a handful of mature plants in both America and Europe.

ORIGIN Arid areas of Afghanistan, Pakistan, Saudi Arabia, Iran.
MATURE HEIGHT To 20ft.
TRUNK Multiple, sometimes prostrate, as if too heavy to support itself, sometimes erect, sometimes branched; about 12in in diameter.
LEAF Stiff, fan-shaped leaf, costapalmate, blue gray in color.
FLOWER STALK Flowering is terminal, but does not result in the death of the plant, as the next fork down takes over.
FRUIT ¾in in diameter, red brown when ripe.
SEED Round, ½in in diameter, very hard, with a small central cavity.
CULTIVATION The seeds, given adequate heat, begin to germinate rapidly, but this process may continue over many months. *OUTDOORS* Hot, dry and bright would summarize this palm's requirements. A well-drained soil, but with an adequate supply of water is also beneficial. It is extremely cold-tolerant, a feature largely due to its desert habitat. *INDOORS* It would probably make a good conservatory subject, as it thrives in hot, dry air, and bright light.

NEODYPSIS DECARYI
TRIANGLE PALM

An instantly recognizable palm, it is rapidly gaining in popularity, but becoming rare in its native home due to excessive seed exports.

ORIGIN Madagascar.
MATURE HEIGHT To 20ft.
TRUNK The leaf bases form a unique triangular shape at the top of the trunk; below this, the trunks is conventionally round, about 12in in diameter.
LEAF Long and elegant, a silvery green in color, feather-shaped, and drooping at the tips, forming three distinct ranks even on young plants; the new spear is covered with a dark reddish-brown velvet, as on deer's antlers.
FLOWER STALK From among the leaf bases.
FRUIT ¾in, oval.
SEED ½in in diameter, round.
CULTIVATION This is a wonderful palm for both indoor and outdoor use. *OUTDOORS* Extremely drought-tolerant, it should be grown in full sun. Shade-grown specimens tend to be very attenuated and are much less attractive. Be careful not to over-fertilize, as this leads to rapid browning of the leaf tips. *INDOORS* An unsurpassed palm for indoor use, it tolerates low to medium light (though it prefers brighter, indirect light). Its triangular shape means that it can easily be stood against a wall, or in a corner.

NORMANBYA NORMANBYI
BLACK PALM

A beautiful Australian native, it has plumose leaves like bottle brushes.
ORIGIN Tropical northeastern Australia.
MATURE HEIGHT To 50ft.
TRUNK Slim, gray, composed of a very hard black wood, from which it gets its name; crownshaft.
LEAF Attractive and plumose (leaflets at different angles to the leaf stem); wide and coarse leaflets.
FLOWER STALK From below the crownshaft.
FRUIT Egg-shaped, 1½in long, beautiful pink color when ripe.
SEED Round at one end, pointed at the other.
CULTIVATION Some seeds germinate very quickly if fresh, but often there is a low success rate. *OUTDOORS* The black palm requires tropical to subtropical habitat, rich soil, and plenty of water in dry periods. *INDOORS* Although not much tried, it shows promise as a house plant. Humidity must be maintained.

NYPA FRUTICANS
NIPAH PALM

This palm is so different from all the others that for a long time it was not considered to be a palm at all. It is commonly seen in the tropics, where it lines coast and river.
ORIGIN Coastal, swampy, tropical areas from India to Australia.
MATURE HEIGHT To 25ft.
TRUNK Subterranean, or indeed submarine, sometimes forking.
LEAF Very long and erect, feather-shaped, with a strong, round leaf stalk.
FLOWER STALK A unique vertically held structure, like a football on a stalk.
FRUIT Much like those of *Pandanus* species, roughly wedge-shaped, so that all the seeds can fit together in a ball shape; 3in long.
SEED Covered in fiber, walnut-sized, and edible.
CULTIVATION Culture away from their native home seems to present difficulties; the seeds either refuse to germinate, or die soon afterwards. *OUTDOORS* Tropical, marshy conditions are required, with deep mud, or soft soil. This palm tolerates brackish water. *INDOORS* A plant might succeed in a hot and humid greenhouse, but it would otherwise be extremely difficult to grow this atypical palm indoors.

ONCOSPERMA HORRIDUM

Distinctive, tropical, tall, clumping palms, they are extremely spiny in all their parts.

ORIGIN Malaysia, Indonesia.

MATURE HEIGHT To 70ft.

TRUNK Multiple, slim, dark, covered in sharp spines, the clump being quite impossible to penetrate.

LEAF Feather-shaped and elegant, the leaflets are held flat.

FLOWER STALK From among the leaf bases.

FRUIT ½in in diameter, black when ripe.

SEED Small, round.

CULTIVATION The seeds lose their viability very quickly, and need to be planted within days of collection. *OUTDOORS* An attractive palm for tropical locations, it forms a large clump in time. Its spiny nature may be a problem. *INDOORS* It is not known to be used indoors, but tropical conditions would undoubtedly be required.

ONCOSPERMA TIGILLARIUM
NIBUNG PALM

A tall, elegant, clumping palm for the tropics, it is spiny in all its parts, which may prove a deterrent to its use.

ORIGIN Southeast Asia.

MATURE HEIGHT To 80ft.

TRUNK Multiple, with as many as 40 or 50 trunks to a clump; trunks are slim and covered in sharp black spines.

LEAF Elegant feather-shaped leaf, with the leaflets drooping down both sides of the leaf stalk, which is also covered in spines.

FLOWER STALK From among the leaf bases, spiny.

FRUIT ¾in in circumference, black or dark blue when ripe, with a white bloom.

SEED Small, round.

CULTIVATION The seeds need to be absolutely fresh for successful germination, which takes two or three months. *OUTDOORS* This is a large and impressive palm for the moist tropics, but care should be taken in public areas, because of the sharp spines. *INDOORS* It is unlikely to succeed in anything other than a humid greenhouse.

ORANIOPSIS APPENDICULATA

A little known but interesting palm, it was believed until recently to be related to *Orania;* however, it is now known to be closer to *Ceroxylon.* It will undoubtedly become more widespread in the future.

ORIGIN Queensland, Australia, where it grows in dense rainforests.

MATURE HEIGHT To 30ft, but very slow-growing.

TRUNK Rather thick and stout, up to 24in through, with clear rings, the scars left by old leaves, which drop cleanly.

LEAF Feather-shaped, held vertical or horizontal, but not drooping, dark green upper surface and silvery underneath.

FLOWER STALK From among the leaf bases.

FRUIT Round, 1½in in diameter, yellow when ripe.

SEED Large and round.

CULTIVATION Not much notice was taken of this palm until quite recently, when its relationship to *Ceroxylon* was noted, and thus not much is known of its cultural requirements. The seeds are very slow to germinate, and subsequent growth is also extremely slow. *OUTDOORS* It seems to prefer shade, and a situation that is cool and humid. Given this, it should do well in a subtropical or warm temperate location, but is very slow. *INDOORS* Nothing is known of its indoor requirements.

PARAJUBAEA COCOIDES

An exciting and beautiful palm from South America, it is very fast-growing, resembling a coconut, but much more cold-tolerant. The main problems seem to be firstly, to obtain the seeds, and then to get them to germinate.

ORIGIN Ecuador, where it is quite common, but only in cultivation; not now known in the wild, but thought to come from the Andean slopes.

MATURE HEIGHT To 40ft.

TRUNK Slim, ringed with old leaf scars.

LEAF Attractive feather leaf, with shiny dark green leaflets, silvery underneath.

FLOWER STALK From among the leaf bases.

FRUIT 1½in, dark green; brown when ripe.

SEED 1¼in long, with three prominent crests at one end.

CULTIVATION The large seeds germinate erratically and with some difficulty. Success is claimed for various techniques, such as alternating day/night temperatures, cracking the hard seed coat, bathing the seeds in pure oxygen on a bed of moist sphagnum moss, or any combination of the above. Once germinated, growth is very fast. *OUTDOORS* Temperate, frost-free conditions suit this palm best, with a position in full sun. It requires cool nights and sunny days, simulating its mountainous home. *INDOORS* It is said to stop growing after the root has made a few circles around the pot, and is certainly more happy in the ground.

PELAGODOXA HENRYANA

A beautiful but extremely rare palm from the South Pacific, it is not dissimilar to *Phoenicophorium*.

ORIGIN The Marquesas Islands, surely the quintessential South Pacific group; it is rare in the wild, and not common even in tropical botanic gardens.

MATURE HEIGHT To 20ft.

TRUNK Slim, solitary, perhaps 6in in diameter.

LEAF Large, simple and entire, except when split by the wind.

FLOWER STALK Among the leaf bases.

FRUIT Large – the size of a tennis ball – and distinctively warty and corky.

SEED About 1in in diameter, smooth.

CULTIVATION As can be imagined, not much is known about this rare palm, but certainly humid and tropical conditions would be required. The seeds are slow and erratic to germinate. *OUTDOORS* Likely to succeed only in the tropics, it will hopefully become more available in the years to come. *INDOORS* It is not known to have been tried indoors.

PHOENICOPHORIUM BORSIGIANUM

A beautiful, simple-leaved palm similar in many respects to the foregoing *Pelagodoxa*, it is easily distinguished by its seeds and toothed leaflet tips.

ORIGIN Seychelles Islands, Indian Ocean.

MATURE HEIGHT To 40ft.

TRUNK Slim and solitary, covered with spines when young.

LEAF Simple, entire, but subject to damage by the wind, which causes the leaves to split; lthe tips of the leaves are toothed.

FLOWER STALK From among the leaf bases.

FRUIT About ½in long, and heart shaped.

SEED Slightly smaller, similarly shaped, covered with a few distinctive veins.

CULTIVATION The small seeds germinate well, if very fresh, but quickly lose all viability. *OUTDOORS* Tropical and humid conditions are required. This is not an easy palm to grow, but worth persevering with. *INDOORS* It is not known to be used as a house plant, though it can be grown in a tropical greenhouse, with high humidity.

PHOENIX CANARIENSIS
CANARY ISLAND DATE PALM

One of the most widespread palms in the world, and very common everywhere in warm temperate areas, ranging from the south of France, to Australia and California.

ORIGIN The Canary Islands, off the west coast of Africa.
MATURE HEIGHT To 60ft, usually seen much less.
TRUNK Solitary and very stout, up to 3ft in diameter, covered with distinctive old leaf scars which form diamond-shaped patterns.
LEAF Mid-green, feather-shaped, with valley-, as opposed to roof-shaped, leaflets, which is distinctive of the entire genus; the lower leaflets are developed into long and extremely stiff and sharp spines, which are quite dangerous when handling the plants.
FLOWER STALK From among the leaf bases.
FRUIT To 2in long and ½in wide, orange when ripe; inedible.
SEED Typical date-stone shape, but with rounded ends.
CULTIVATION With heat, the seeds germinate easily and quickly, generally within a few weeks. *OUTDOORS* An essential, though perhaps over-used, palm for warm temperate zones, it grows quickly, but requires a lot of space to develop fully. It is tolerant of cold and drought, but prefers full sun. *INDOORS* An excellent indoor palm, with a spiky, architectural appearance, it thrives in bright, indirect light, and tolerates dry air well.

PHOENIX RECLINATA
SENEGAL DATE PALM, AFRICAN DATE PALM

This is a beautiful, clump-forming date palm, the trunks of which lean outward, hence the name.

ORIGIN Equatorial Africa.
MATURE HEIGHT To 30ft.
TRUNK Multiple, slim, covered with old leaf scars; *reclinata* refers to the outward-leaning habit of the trunks.
LEAF Not dissimilar to that of *P. canariensis*, but only about half as long.
FLOWER STALK From among the leaf bases.
FRUIT Oval in shape, about ¾in long; brown when ripe.
SEED ½in long, grooved, round ended.
CULTIVATION This tropical palm will also succeed in warm temperate areas, but does not like frost and cold. The seeds sprout easily and quickly. *OUTDOORS* A beautiful clumping palm, it is tough and tolerant. *INDOORS* Although undoubtedly suitable, when a young plant, for indoor use, it has not been much tried.

PHOENIX DACTYLIFERA

This useful palm is widespread throughout the Middle East and the drier tropics, and its fruit, the well-known date, has been harvested for centuries. Dates can be dried, and kept without deterioration for long periods of time. The male and female flowers are on separate trees, but the males produce pollen in such huge quantities that only one male tree is required for every 100 females. During the season when pollen is produced, the slightest breeze can waft clouds and clouds of pollen, like a yellow mist, drifting across the sand. A good female tree can produce up to 45kg/100lb of fruit per year, and palm wine – "toddy" – can be produced from the sap collected from unopened flower stalks. Commercially, date palms are produced from the suckers which readily sprout from the base of the tree.

PHOENIX DACTYLIFERA
DATE PALM

This is the date palm of commerce, grown by the million in Middle Eastern countries, and elsewhere, for its delicious and abundant fruit.

ORIGIN North Africa.

MATURE HEIGHT To 80ft.

TRUNK To 12in in diameter, covered with rough old leaf scars; often seen damaged or distorted; produces suckers freely when allowed, but these are generally removed, leaving a solitary trunk.

LEAF Feather-shaped, like *Phoenix canariensis,* but leaflets stiffer, coarser and fewer with a distinctive gray green coloration.

FLOWER STALK From among the leaf bases.

FRUIT The well-known date; many varieties have been developed.

SEED Long and narrow, grooved, with pointed ends.

CULTIVATION The date palm is easily grown from seed, which germinates well and readily, usually within a few weeks of sowing. Alternatively, it can be grown from suckers removed from the parent plant. *OUTDOORS* Although not as cold-tolerant as *P. canariensis,* it is easily grown in warm temperate areas. The sexes are on separate trees. *INDOORS* It is just as suitable as *P. canariensis* for indoor-growing, but its foliage is harder and less attractive.

PHOENIX ROEBELENII
PYGMY DATE PALM

A comparatively small-growing date palm, it is very popular for indoor use, forming a perfect miniature palm tree.
ORIGIN Laos, in Southeast Asia.
MATURE HEIGHT To only about 10ft.
TRUNK Slim, solitary, only about 3 or 4in in diameter; sometimes the old leaf bases project in a distinctive fashion, like pegs.
LEAF Feather-shaped; the leaflets much softer than those of all the other phoenix palms, though the lower ones still form sharp spines.
FLOWER STALK From among the leaf bases.
FRUIT Small, about ½in long, brown when ripe.
SEED Typical date stone shape.
CULTIVATION The small seeds germinate readily, generally within six to eight weeks of sowing. *OUTDOORS* A perfect palm for the smaller property, it grows in tropical, subtropical and warm temperate zones. *INDOORS* It is an equally wonderful palm for indoors, where it tolerates low light and abuse, but prefers bright indirect light. Sometimes a lack of iron can cause the leaves to turn yellow. It also looks good on a deck in the warmer months.

PHOENIX RUPICOLA
CLIFF DATE PALM

Arguably the most attractive of all the date palms, it has a graceful habit and glossy leaflets, which are much finer than those of the other phoenix palms, with the exception of *P. roebelenii*.
ORIGIN India.
MATURE HEIGHT To 25ft.
TRUNK Slim, solitary, with scars left by old leaves.
LEAF Feather-shaped, and flat, with glossy leaflets; sometimes the leaves are twisted so they are perpendicular to the ground.
FLOWER STALK From among the leaf bases.
FRUIT ¾in long, dark red when ripe.
SEED ½in long, narrow, grooved along its length.
CULTIVATION The seeds germinate easily and readily. *OUTDOORS* This palm grows in a wide range of climates, from tropical to warm temperate. Lots of water in dry weather will be much appreciated and will help the palm to look its best. *INDOORS* It is not much used as a house plant, but there is no reason why it should not succeed.

PHOENIX THEOPHRASTII
CRETAN DATE PALM

This recently described palm is one of only two species native to Europe, the other being *Chamaerops humilis*, the Mediterranean fan palm. The Cretan date palm should be more widely grown, as it is a handsome plant, and should be moderately hardy to cold-tolerant.
ORIGIN Crete, and the western edge of Turkey.
MATURE HEIGHT To about 20ft.
TRUNK Clumping, slim, covered with old leaf scars.
LEAF Feather-shaped, sometimes an attractive silvery gray green.
FLOWER STALK From among the leaf bases.
FRUIT ¾in long, dark brown when ripe.
SEED ½in long, shaped like other phoenix seeds, with a groove along the length.
CULTIVATION It is easily grown from seed, which germinates readily. *OUTDOORS* A palm for the temperate areas of the world, where it requires full sun, and permanent access to ground water. It should be moderately frost-tolerant. *INDOORS* It has not been tried as a house plant, but should succeed in a brightly lit position.

PIGAFETTA FILARIS
WANGA PALM

A very fast-growing tropical palm, it seems to have discovered its own ecological niche in disturbed soil, often at the sides of new roads or where rainforest trees have been cut down. This would suggest that it needs bright light to succeed.
ORIGIN Confined to a few isolated islands in Southeast Asia.
MATURE HEIGHT Tall, up to 150ft.
TRUNK Sometimes over 12in in diameter, closely ringed.
LEAF Elegantly recurved feather leaf, the base of which is covered with light brown spines; these form horizontal narrow stripes in a very distinctive fashion.
FLOWER STALK From among the lower leaves.
FRUIT Small, no more than ½in long, covered with pretty scales, like snakeskin.
SEED Small and oval.
CULTIVATION The small seeds need to be planted immediately, as they lose their viability extremely quickly, possibly within days. *OUTDOORS* This is a beautiful palm for a tropical location, but will probably not succeed elsewhere. Plant it in a sunny position, and never allow the plant to dry out. *INDOORS* It would be difficult to keep indoors, even in a humid greenhouse, but worth a try if enough light could be provided for the young seedling.

PINANGA CORONATA

One of a genus containing well over 100 species, it is commonly seen in forests and undergrowth of its native home.

ORIGIN Mainly confined to Malaysia, and some neighbouring countries.

MATURE HEIGHT To 15ft.

TRUNK Multiple, clustered, slim and green, with prominent rings and a crownshaft.

LEAF A feather leaf, broad for its length.

FLOWER STALK From below the lowest leaves.

FRUIT Small, shiny and bright red; black when ripe.

SEED Small, pointed at one end.

CULTIVATION *Pinangas* mainly require tropical conditions, though some species show a certain tolerance to cold. *OUTDOORS* A shady protected spot in the humid tropics would suit this attractive palm best. Provide plenty of water in dry weather. *INDOORS Pinangas* show some promise as indoor plants if attention is paid to humidity and warmth, which should be gentle and constant. Young plants often have mottled leaves.

PINANGA KUHLII
IVORY CANE PALM

Another attractive *pinanga*, it has mottled leaves, especially as a young plant. Sometimes sold as a house plant, it is commonly grown in the tropics, and can generally be seen in botanic gardens there.

ORIGIN Indonesia.

MATURE HEIGHT To 25ft.

TRUNK Multiple, clumping, slim, elegant, green, ringed.

LEAF Feather-shaped, with few, broad leaflets; these are often attractively mottled, especially in juvenile plants.

FLOWER STALK From below the crownshaft.

FRUIT ½in long, bright red when ripe.

SEED Oval.

CULTIVATION The ivory cane palm is easily grown from seed, which needs to be very fresh to germinate. *OUTDOORS* This species is rather more cold-tolerant than many others in the genus, however it still requires at least warm temperate conditions to succeed. *INDOORS* It may be tried indoors – the beautiful mottled foliage of the young plants makes worthwhile any special efforts required to provide warmth and humidity.

PRITCHARDIA PACIFICA
FIJI FAN PALM

For many, this is the ultimate tropical palm, and the very essence of the tropics.

ORIGIN Fiji.

MATURE HEIGHT To 30ft.

TRUNK Solitary, about 12in in diameter.

LEAF Beautiful, stiff, fan-shaped leaf, deeply pleated and light green in colour.

FLOWER STALK From among the leaves.

FRUIT ½in in diameter, black when ripe.

SEED Round, small.

CULTIVATION This palm is easily grown from seed, which germinates in a few weeks. *OUTDOORS* Tropical or subtropical conditions suit this palm best, together with an abundance of water in dry weather. They are often seen with yellow discoloration of the leaves, which may be a nutrient deficiency. *INDOORS* Not really suitable as a house plant, it may be grown for a few years in a humid greenhouse.

PTYCHOSPERMA ELEGANS
SOLITAIRE PALM

One of the most commonly seen of its genus, it has a solitary trunk.

ORIGIN Northeastern Australia.

MATURE HEIGHT To 30ft.

TRUNK Slim, solitary, gray, ringed with old leaf scars; crownshaft.

LEAF Feather-shaped, with fairly broad leaflets, the ends of which look as though they have been nibbled.

FLOWER STALK From below the crownshaft.

FRUIT Borne in large numbers, about ¾in long, red when ripe.

SEED Distinctive, with grooves running along its length.

CULTIVATION The seeds germinate quickly and easily, usually within a few weeks of sowing, but need to be fresh for good results. *OUTDOORS* An attractive, small palm for tropical and humid locations, it appreciates plenty of water in dry weather. *INDOORS* They are often seen in planting schemes in shopping malls and similar locations where, if bright light and enough humidity can be maintained, they do well.

PTYCHOSPERMA
MACARTHURII
MACARTHUR PALM

A clumping *ptychosperma*, it is a common sight in botanic gardens throughout the tropics. The bright red fruits, freely borne, make it easy to identify.

ORIGIN Northeast Australia.

MATURE HEIGHT To 25ft.

TRUNK Multiple and clustering, slim, and ringed with old leaf scars; crownshaft.

LEAF Feather-shaped, the fairly regular and broad leaflets having jagged ends.

FLOWER STALK From below the crownshaft.

FRUIT Bright red when ripe, about ¾in long.

SEED Grooved along its length, in typical *ptychosperma* fashion.

CULTIVATION Seeds that are fresh will sprout within a few weeks of planting. *OUTDOORS* A useful palm for the tropical garden, it occupies the minimum amount of space, but provides an attractive shape and color. *INDOORS* It may certainly be tried indoors, but attention must be paid to levels of warmth and humidity.

RAPHIA FARINIFERA
RAFFIA PALM

This genus of palms has the longest leaves of any plants in the vegetable kingdom – up to 60ft long. They were often used in the past for the production of raffia string, but this has lessened with the greater use of man-made materials.

ORIGIN Madagascar.

MATURE HEIGHT To 70ft, much of this being taken up by the leaves, which grow on comparatively short trunks.

TRUNK Multiple; each trunk grows only to about 10ft and 12in or more in diameter; the trunk dies after fruiting, but is replaced by others.

LEAF Among the longest in the plant kingdom; a massive feather-shaped leaf up to 60ft long, held erect.

FLOWER STALK A massive structure that hangs down from the leaves.

FRUIT Large, up to 3in long, and covered with attractive scales.

SEED 1½in long, grooved and furrowed.

CULTIVATION The large seeds seem difficult to germinate, and would certainly have to be fresh for success. *OUTDOORS* Swampy ground in the humid tropics would suit this massive, water-loving palm admirably. Much space would be required to appreciate its size and beauty. *INDOORS* It is not known to be used indoors, where lack of humidity and light would undoubtedly be limiting factors.

RAVENEA RIVULARIS
MAJESTY PALM

An exciting "new" palm, it is becoming famous for its fast growth, and tolerance of cool conditions.

ORIGIN Madagascar.

MATURE HEIGHT To 40ft.

TRUNK 12in or more in diameter.

LEAF An elegant feather-shaped leaf, which clasps the trunk in a distinctive manner.

FLOWER STALK From among the leaves.

FRUIT ½in in diameter, round.

SEED Small, round.

CULTIVATION The small seeds germinate easily, but only if absolutely fresh, as they lose their viability very quickly. *OUTDOORS* A beautiful palm for tropics, subtropics and warm temperate areas, it grows extremely quickly. Much water appreciated in dry weather. *INDOORS* This palm, which has only recently been brought into cultivation, seems to thrive indoors, tolerating low light, and growing well, even in comparatively cool conditions.

REINHARDTIA GRACILIS
WINDOW PALM

A tiny, dainty and beautiful palm, it is much in demand as a house plant. The common name refers to the holes, or "windows" in the leaves.

ORIGIN Central America.

MATURE HEIGHT To only 4 or 5ft.

TRUNK Mutliple, very thin, only about 1in in diameter.

LEAF A feather leaf, but with only a few broad leaflets, often with small holes or "windows" at their base.

FLOWER STALK From among the leaves.

FRUIT Small, ½in in circumference, and black when ripe.

SEED Small, round and wrinkled.

CULTIVATION The small seeds germinate quite easily if fresh. *OUTDOORS* A position in a tropical location that is protected from both sun and wind would suit these small palms best, together with an abundance of water in dry weather. *INDOORS* These splendid house plants are difficult to grow, but worth any special effort. Protect them from direct light, and pay attention to the humidity.

RHAPIDOPHYLLUM HYSTRIX
NEEDLE PALM

Certainly the most cold-tolerant palm known, it will survive incredibly low temperatures, but requires summer heat to grow well.

ORIGIN Southeastern US.

MATURE HEIGHT To 7 or 8ft only, and as wide.

TRUNK The short trunk may be underground, or grow to a few feet above ground. It suckers very freely and unless trimmed the plant grows into a dense, impenetrable bush. The trunks are covered with vertical, sharp, black spines, up to 4in long, among which the seeds drop, often germinating there and then dying for lack of water and nutrients.

LEAF Fan-shaped, dark glossy green above, paler beneath.

FLOWER STALK Almost lost among the leaf bases and spines.

FRUIT ¾in long, ovoid in shape.

SEED ½in long, grooved down one side.

CULTIVATION The seeds are difficult to obtain and erratic to germinate. *OUTDOORS* This palm grows best in warm temperate areas with good hot summers, and can be planted either in shade or full sun. In cooler areas they grow slowly, and require a sunny position. This is one of the few truly hardy palms. *INDOORS* It is not known to have been tried indoors.

RHAPIS EXCELSA
LADY PALM

This is possibly the perfect indoor palm, tolerating low light-levels, and growing slowly to an impressive size over a number of years.

ORIGIN Southern China.

MATURE HEIGHT To 10ft.

TRUNK Multiple, very slim, covered in dark woven fibers; forms a large clump or bush, with leaves all the way down to the ground.

LEAF Fan-shaped, deeply cut, dark glossy green in color, the ends of the leaflets are squared off and jagged.

FLOWER STALK From among the leaf bases, towards the top of the plant.

FRUIT Small, ½in in diameter.

SEED Small and round.

CULTIVATION The small seeds are easy to germinate, but the young seedlings grow extremely slowly. Plants may also be grown from suckers from a parent plant. *OUTDOORS* The lady palm will grow in sun or shade, and in tropical, subtropical or warm temperate areas. A very adaptable palm, it shows some tolerance to cold. *INDOORS* Unsurpassed as a house palm, it is extremely tolerant of low light and dry air, though the plants should never be allowed to dry out. Variegated specimens are sometimes available. Possibly the only drawback is their high price, which is related to the plants' slow growth.

RHAPIS HUMILIS
SLENDER LADY PALM

The slender lady palm is similar in general appearance to the foregoing.
All plants in cultivation are grown from suckers, as female plants are not
known. It is not often seen for sale; plants bought as *R. humilis* often
turn out to be a third species, *R. subtilis,* which is much more tropical.
ORIGIN Not known for certain, but likely to be China.
MATURE HEIGHT To 12ft.
TRUNK Slim, multiple, again covered in woven dark fibers.
LEAF Generally similar to those of *R. excelsa,* but the leaflet tips are
pointed, instead of being squared off; the leaflets are also narrower, and
more numerous.
FLOWER STALK Male only, from among the leaf bases, towards the top
of the plants.
FRUIT Not known to exist; seeds offered as R. humilis are almost
certain to be another species of *rhapis,* or, worse, another species of
palm.
SEED See above.
CULTIVATION This species must be propagated vegetatively, that is,
from suckers. *OUTDOORS* Plants will grow in a wide range of climates
and conditions, in shade or sun, though they certainly look more
refreshed in shade. *INDOORS* An excellent indoor species, it will put up
with low light and general abuse. Do not, however, allow the soil
to dry out.

RHOPALOSTYLIS SAPIDA
NIKAU OR SHAVING-BRUSH PALM

Easily recognizable by its swollen, almost round crownshaft, this
species is native to New Zealand.
ORIGIN New Zealand.
MATURE HEIGHT To 25ft.
TRUNK Solitary, about 8 or 9in in diameter, with a prominent
crownshaft, which, together with the erect leaves, gives it its common
name of shaving-brush palm.
LEAF Feather-shaped, leaflets pointed, with prominent veins.
FLOWER STALK From below the crownshaft.
FRUIT ¾in in diameter, red when ripe.
SEED ½in in diameter, one side carries a scar.
CULTIVATION The seeds take two or three months to germinate and
seedling growth is quite slow. *OUTDOORS* The nikau prefers a cool,
shady, moist location, definitely out of direct sunlight. Rich soil and an
abundance of water will result in quite steady growth, even in temperate
areas. However, *R. sapida* is only cold-tolerant down to − 24°F, and it
must be protected if colder weather threatens. It is one of the few hardy
feather palms. *INDOORS* Not known to be used as a house plant, it
shows some promise, however, in view of its preference for low light.

ROYSTONEA ELATA
FLORIDA ROYAL PALM

One of several species much planted as ornamentals in tropical countries, it is easily recognized by the huge, towering, almost white trunks and glossy green crownshafts.

ORIGIN Florida.

MATURE HEIGHT To 80ft.

TRUNK Solitary, thick, pale gray to white, with a prominent green crownshaft.

LEAF Plumose (like a bottle brush), and with a feather-shaped leaf.

FLOWER STALK From below the crownshaft, erect.

FRUIT Small and round, perhaps ½in in diameter.

SEED Small and round; somehow it seems curious that such a massive tree could grow from such a small seed.

CULTIVATION The seeds germinate easily and rapidly. *OUTDOORS* Consider long and hard before deciding where to plant this large and beautiful tropical tree, as it will certainly dominate the landscape for many years to come. Often seen in avenues in the tropics, they make remarkably even growth. *INDOORS* Although not much tried indoors, it would probably be possible to grow it for a few years, if attention were paid to humidity and light.

ROYSTONEA REGIA
CUBAN ROYAL PALM

This is closely related to the foregoing, and usually distinguishable by the trunk. However, since individuals can be so variable, this is not a reliable means of identification.

ORIGIN Cuba.

MATURE HEIGHT To 70ft, less than *R. elata*.

TRUNK Massive, pale gray or whitish, often bulging at the base and again in the middle section; prominent green crownshaft.

LEAF Feather-shaped, leaflets at different angles.

FLOWER STALK From below the crownshaft, erect.

FRUIT Small, ½in in diameter.

SEED Small, round and insignificant.

CULTIVATION This palm is easily grown from seed, which germinates readily. *OUTDOORS* A tropical palm, it requires full sun and plenty of water in dry weather. *INDOORS* This is not used as a house plant, but it would be possible to use it this way for a few years.

SABAL MINOR
BLUE OR DWARF PALMETTO PALM

A fairly low-growing, trunkless *sabal*, it is extremely cold-hardy, though it needs summer heat to grow well.
ORIGIN Southeastern USA.
MATURE HEIGHT To 12ft.
TRUNK Trunkless, or with an underground stem, sometimes rising a few feet above ground.
LEAF Very stiff, blue green, fan-shaped leaf, which is costapalmate (the leaf stem continues into the leaf).
FLOWER STALK From among the leaves and rising to perhaps twice the height of the plant.
FRUIT Small, ½in in circumference, black when ripe.
SEED Small, round, slightly flattened, and a glossy dark red brown.
CULTIVATION The blue palm is easily grown from seed, which germinates quickly. *OUTDOORS* Requiring full sun, in tropical to temperate zones, this palm needs much heat to succeed, although it is extremely hardy to cold, being one of the most cold-hardy palms, in fact. It prefers swampy ground, and is slow-growing. *INDOORS* It may be grown indoors, but requires very bright light; lack of humidity is not, however, a problem.

SABAL PALMETTO
PALMETTO PALM

A tall-growing *sabal*, this is Florida's state tree.
ORIGIN Southeastern USA.
MATURE HEIGHT To 80ft.
TRUNK Solitary, up to 18in in diameter, usually less; older part of the trunk smooth, but above that, it is covered with old leaf bases which are split into two in a distinctive fashion.
LEAF Stiff, green, costapalmate.
FLOWER STALK From among the leaf bases.
FRUIT Small, ½in in diameter, black when ripe.
SEED Small, round and slightly flattened.
CULTIVATION Easily germinated, the small seeds sprout in a few weeks. *OUTDOORS* This is an interesting palm for the tropics and subtropics, where it grows quickly. The old leaves hang down and should be trimmed back for a neat appearance. *INDOORS* Not much used as a house plant, it would certainly be possible to keep this palm in a high-light situation.

SERENOA REPENS
SAW PALMETTO

A small palm, it is native to Florida and the surrounding areas, where it covers huge areas of land. Silver and blue forms are sometimes seen.
ORIGIN Southeastern USA.
MATURE HEIGHT To 8 or 9ft, usually much less.
TRUNK Usually underground, or at best, only a few feet tall; clump forming.
LEAF Stiff, small, fan-shaped, silver, blue or green.
FLOWER STALK From among the leaves.
FRUIT ¾in long, oval, black when ripe.
SEED ½in long.
CULTIVATION The seeds germinate easily, though this may take several weeks. Plants may also be reproduced from suckers. *OUTDOORS* Full sun is best, together with adequate moisture, and a tropical to temperate climate. This species shows some tolerance of cold. *INDOORS* Although it is not known as a house plant, it might be worth any special effort to grow this attractive small palm. Dry air is unlikely to be a problem, but insufficient light might cause difficulties.

SYAGRUS ROMANZOFFIANA
QUEEN PALM

Well known and popular, it was until recently known as *Arecastrum romanzoffianum*, and prior to that *Cocos plumosa*, by which name it may still be found for sale in some plant centers.
ORIGIN Brazil.
MATURE HEIGHT To 60ft.
TRUNK Solitary, and ringed with old leaf bases; no crownshaft.
LEAF Plumose, that is, with the leaflets radiating at different angles.
FLOWER STALK From among the leaf bases.
FRUIT To 1in long, yellow when ripe.
SEED ¾in long, covered in fibers.
CULTIVATION This palm is germinated from seed, and the first simple leaves can be up to 3ft or more long. *OUTDOORS* It will grow in a wide range of climates, from tropical to temperate, and appreciates much water and fertilizer. It grows very fast, and shows some tolerance to cold. *INDOORS* Indoor cultivation is possible, given sufficient light levels.

TRACHYCARPUS FORTUNEI

The common name "Chusan palm" derives from the fact that it was on Chusan Island – or Chou-Shan or Zhoushan as it's now known – that Robert Fortune, the famous 19th-century plant hunter, first saw the palm that was to bear his name. However, the trees he saw were more than likely cultivated specimens. Zhoushan Island is in the East China Sea, off Hangzhou (Hangchow), south of Shanghai, and at one time it was to have been the main British settlement in the area. However, the final choice was another tiny island – Hong Kong – and the rest is history.

TRACHYCARPUS FORTUNEI
CHUSAN PALM

This is perhaps the most popular palm for cooler climates, where it grows well with the minimum of care and attention, and is extremely hardy to cold, frost and snow. An attractive form called *T. wagnerianus* has much smaller, stiffer leaves, particularly apparent in young plants, but is certainly not a distinct species. In the United States, this form is often mis-named *T. takil.*

ORIGIN China; *Trachycarpus takil*, probably only another form, comes from the western Indian Himalayas.
MATURE HEIGHT To 40ft.
TRUNK Slim, solitary, covered with old leaf bases, and brown fibrous matted hairy fibers; if not trimmed, the old leaves hang down in the manner of *Washingtonia*. In some countries, the fibers are stripped as a matter of course, leaving a bare trunk, so the hairy trunk should not be considered a reliable identifying feature.
LEAF Fan shaped, 4ft across, irregularly divided.
FLOWER STALK From among the lower leaves, yellow.
FRUIT Kidney-shaped, about ½in long, a blue black when ripe, with a white bloom.
SEED Kidney-shaped.
CULTIVATION The seeds germinate easily within a few weeks of sowing. *OUTDOORS* This is a plant for temperate to warm temperate zones, but unhappy in the tropics. It prefers a heavy rich clay soil, and hates both wind, which damages the leaves, and waterlogged soil. It is very cold-hardy. *INDOORS* It may be grown as a house plant for a few years, but is much happier as a tub plant on the deck, or in the ground.

THRINAX FLORIDANA
FLORIDA THATCH PALM

This is one of a number of species occurring in the West Indies, Central America and Florida.
ORIGIN Florida Keys.
MATURE HEIGHT To 30ft.
TRUNK Slim, solitary, and lacking a crownshaft.
LEAF Fan-shaped, or sometimes forming almost a complete circle; the leaf segments are cut to about half the depth of the leaf.
FLOWER STALK From among the leaf bases.
FRUIT Small and round, perhaps ½in in diameter.
SEED ¼in in diameter.
CULTIVATION The small seeds germinate easily and readily.
OUTDOORS A position in full sun would suit these drought-tolerant palms best. *INDOORS* It is not known to be used as an indoor plant.

TRACHYCARPUS MARTIANUS

Quite different from *T. fortunei,* this elegant species has a naturally bare trunk, and differs in leaf and seed details.
ORIGIN Eastern Himalayas in northern India, southern Burma, and Assam.
MATURE HEIGHT To 40ft.
TRUNK Slim, solitary, usually bare except for the area immediately below the crown; sometimes covered with old leaves in the manner of *Washingtonia.*
LEAF Fan-shaped, regularly divided to about halfway, glossy, and mid-green in color.
FLOWER STALK From among the leaf bases; flowers are white, as opposed to yellow.
FRUIT Oval in shape, ½in long.
SEED Oval, grooved down one side like a date seed.
CULTIVATION The seeds germinate readily within two to three months of sowing. The young seedlings seem prone to all manner of pests and should be given preventative treatment. *OUTDOORS* Warm temperate to temperate conditions would seem best for this beautiful but rarely grown palm. It is less cold-hardy than its cousin, and more effort should be made to introduce it to botanic as well as private gardens. *INDOORS* This species seems to be vulnerable to attack by every known insect pest. As with seedlings, treat as a preventative rather than as a cure.

TRACHYCARPUS NANUS

The third and last species in the *Trachycarpus* genus, this one does not grow a trunk. Though it is recorded as being locally common in its home country, it has never been brought into cultivation and has only recently even been photographed.
ORIGIN Southwestern China.
MATURE HEIGHT To perhaps 4ft.
TRUNK Either trunkless, or with an underground stem.
LEAF Fan-shaped and stiffly held.
FLOWER STALK From among the leaf bases, erect.
FRUIT Apparently similar to *T. fortunei,* that is, ½in long, kidney-shaped, blue black when ripe, with a white bloom.
SEED Kidney-shaped.
CULTIVATION Nothing is known of the germination or cultural requirements of this palm.

TRITHRINAX ACANTHACOMA
SPINY FIBER PALM

The unattractive common name describes a most attractive palm, which grows in a wide range of climates, and is gradually becoming more popular, the spines on the trunk being a possible deterrent to its use. It is easily mistaken for *Trachycarpus fortunei* at a distance.
ORIGIN Brazil.
MATURE HEIGHT To 20ft.
TRUNK Solitary, covered with old leaf bases and an intricate pattern of fibers and sharp spines, somewhat dangerous to the touch.
LEAF Fan-shaped, green, rather stiff in appearance, with spines at the leaf tips.
FLOWER STALK From among the leaves.
FRUIT 1in in diameter, round, white to pale green when ripe, hanging in large clusters, like grapes.
SEED Round, ½in in diameter.
CULTIVATION The seeds germinate in about eight to ten weeks. *OUTDOORS* This is an interesting palm for warm temperate to temperate zones, and it shows some tolerance to cold. It is slow-growing, especially in the early stages. *INDOORS* It may be grown as a young plant for a few years, bright light being the main requirement.

TRITHRINAX CAMPESTRIS

An incredibly beautiful, low-growing palm, with multiple stems and the stiffest leaves of any palm. The fact that it is very slow-growing probably accounts for its rarity, even in botanic collections.

ORIGIN Argentina.

MATURE HEIGHT To 6ft, perhaps more.

TRUNK Forms a small clump, with perhaps three or four trunks, about 9 or 10in in diameter, each covered in the most intricate woven fibers and spines, which are incredibly stiff and hard.

LEAF Fan-shaped, about 12–18in long, incredibly stiff and tipped with sharp spines; pale blue, almost white, in color.

FLOWER STALK From among the leaves.

FRUIT Round, ¾in in diameter.

SEED ½in in diameter.

CULTIVATION The small seeds are not easy to germinate, but it is well worth persevering in order to grow this fabulous palm. *OUTDOORS* Because it is so stiff and spiny, it should be planted well away from paths and walkways. Choose a position in full sun, in free-draining soil. Hot, dry and bright conditions are ideal for this palm. *INDOORS* It would probably do very well in a bright conservatory.

VEITCHIA MERRILLII
CHRISTMAS PALM

Often thought to be a miniature royal palm, *Veitchia* is becoming more popular in cultivation, and is often seen in shopping malls and office plantings, as well as for street planting in Florida.

ORIGIN Philippines.

MATURE HEIGHT To 20ft.

TRUNK Solitary, pale, smooth, with indistinct rings; green crownshaft, usually swollen at the base.

LEAF Feather-shaped and recurved, with the leaflets pointing upwards forming a valley-shape; additionally, each leaflet is usually twisted in on itself.

FLOWER STALK From below the crownshaft.

FRUIT About 1in, bright red when ripe and said to resemble Christmas decorations, as they fruit in December.

SEED ½in in circumference.

CULTIVATION Easily grown from seed which germinates, if fresh, within a few weeks of sowing. *OUTDOORS* Tropical and subtropical conditions suit these small palms best, together with an abundance of water. It is quite fast-growing. *INDOORS* This is an attractive plant for interior use, but provide good light and allow the soil to dry out at the surface between thorough waterings.

VERSCHAFFELTIA SPLENDIDA

A beautiful simple-leaved palm, requiring tropical conditions, or a hot and humid greenhouse.

ORIGIN Seychelles Islands.

MATURE HEIGHT To 50ft, but usually much less.

TRUNK Solitary, dark brown, with spines on younger plants; on older trees the trunks are smooth and spineless; stilt roots soon develop, which lift the tree clear of the ground.

LEAF In sheltered locations, the leaves are simple and entire; where it is windy, the leaf usually splits, resulting in a feather shape.

FLOWER STALK From among the leaves.

FRUIT Round, 1in in diameter.

SEED ¾in in diameter, ridged and grooved in an unmistakable fashion; very hard.

CULTIVATION The attractive seeds germinate easily if fresh. *OUTDOORS* For best results, this palm should be planted where it is totally sheltered from wind, in a tropical location. Plenty of water is appreciated. *INDOORS* This is only likely to succeed in a tropical greenhouse, as its demand for humidity is paramount.

WALLICHIA DENSIFLORA

A small clustering palm from the Himalayas, it is fairly hardy to cold, and should be much more widely grown.

ORIGIN The low Himalayas of north India and Assam.

MATURE HEIGHT To 10ft, possibly more.

TRUNK Very short, or non-existent; clump forming.

LEAF Reminiscent of the fishtail palms, with jagged or toothed tips and edges; green above, silvery beneath.

FLOWER STALK From among the leaves.

FRUIT ½in in diameter, oval.

SEED Small, round.

CULTIVATION The small seeds are difficult and erratic to germinate. *OUTDOORS* This will grow in zones ranging from temperate to warm temperate, but is not suitable for the tropics. It will tolerate several degrees of frost, but needs rich soil. *INDOORS* Not known to be grown indoors, it is, however, probably suitable for conservatory use.

WALLICHIA DISTICHA
WALLICH'S PALM

Unfortunately extremely rare in cultivation, this is one of the few truly two-dimensional trees, the leaves growing in one plane, giving a flat appearance from the side, in the manner of the Traveler's palm, *Ravanela madagascariensis.*

ORIGIN Northeast India, Sikkim.

MATURE HEIGHT To 20ft.

TRUNK Solitary, and covered in old leaf bases and fibers.

LEAF The leaves grow in two ranks, erect; leaflets in two planes thus somewhat plumose; an unmistakable formation.

FLOWER STALK From among the leaf bases; flowering is monocarpic, that is, when flowering and fruiting is finished, the tree dies.

FRUIT ¾in in circumference, dark red when ripe.

SEED ½in in diameter, round.

CULTIVATION The seeds are slow and erratic to germinate. *OUTDOORS* Tropical conditions are preferred, with lots of water in dry weather and full sun. *INDOORS* This is not known as an indoor plant.

WASHINGTONIA FILIFERA
CALIFORNIAN COTTON PALM

Very commonly planted in many parts of the world, its popularity is largely due to its fast growth, and consequent cheapness. Established plants show some resistance to cold.

ORIGIN Southwest USA.

MATURE HEIGHT To 60ft.

TRUNK Solitary, up to 2½ft or more thick, sometimes covered with a thick layer of old leaves which may extend down to the ground, though this is often removed to expose the trunk, which is smooth with vertical fissures.

LEAF Fan-shaped, with thread-like fibers between the leaflets.

FLOWER STALK From among the leaves, long and arching out beyond the leaves. This feature distinguishes it from *Livistona australis,* with which it might otherwise be confused.

FRUIT Small, round.

SEED Small, round, dark glossy red.

CULTIVATION The small seeds germinate as easily as grass and are said to have a very long viability, perhaps several years. *OUTDOORS* Temperate to tropical climates suit this adaptable palm, which moves successfully at almost any age. They are drought-resistant and grow best in full sun. *INDOORS* An easy and interesting indoor plant, it requires bright indirect light to flourish.

WASHINGTONIA ROBUSTA
SKYDUSTER

Taller and thinner than the foregoing, this well-named palm grows quickly to an impressive height, and is the palm in the background of all those television crime series shot in Los Angeles.

ORIGIN North Mexico.

MATURE HEIGHT To 100ft.

TRUNK Much thinner and taller than *W. filifera,* but equally likely to be clothed with a thick layer of dead leaves.

LEAF Fan-shaped, perhaps smaller than the foregoing.

FLOWER STALK From among the leaf bases, and longer than the leaves, an important distinguishing feature.

FRUIT Small, round.

SEED Small, round, dark red, glossy.

CULTIVATION The seeds germinate rapidly, within a few weeks, and may be stored for long periods. The desert origin of the *Washingtonias* can be thanked for this. *OUTDOORS* Temperate to tropical areas are home to this fast-growing palm, where it thrives in full sun. Drought-tolerant, it also has the advantage of moving easily at any age. *INDOORS* Another good interior plant, it thrives in bright light, and makes a super conservatory plant for cool climates.

WODYETIA BIFURCATA
FOXTAIL PALM

This is a beautiful and fast-growing Australian palm. *Bifurcata* refers to the fibers on the seeds, which fork in a distinctive fashion.

ORIGIN Northeast Australia.

MATURE HEIGHT To 40ft.

TRUNK Solitary, distinctly ringed, about 9in thick, with crownshaft.

LEAF Plumose, that is, with the leaflets radiating out from the leaf stalk, giving a bottle brush, or foxtail appearance; leaflets fine and narrow.

FLOWER STALK From below the crownshaft.

FRUIT 2in long, oval, red when ripe.

SEED 1½in long, with unique forking fibers.

CULTIVATION The large seeds germinate within two or three months, and subsequent growth is very fast in hot conditions. *OUTDOORS* This drought-tolerant palm grows well in dry soils, but improves markedly with an abundance of water. *INDOORS* Not known to be tried indoors, it would probably be successful if light levels were high enough.

PICTURE CREDITS
. . . .

t = top   b = bottom

All the photographs featured in this book were taken by Martin Gibbons of the Palm Centre, except for the following:

Matthew Baldwin: p43(t), 77(b). Brad Carter: p69(t). Jacquez Deleuze: pp6, 16(b), 26(t), 56(b), 78(t). Bill Dickenson: p43(b). Inge Hoffmann: pp19(b), 37(t), 41(t and b), 52(t). Tony King: pp23(b), 24(t), 34(b), 36(t and b), 42(t), 47, 52(t and b), 68(t), 72(t). David Mclean: p30(x). Sam Mitchell: pp18(b), 27(b), 48(b), 54(t), 58(b). D. S. Neave: p37(b). Parks Department, Durban, South Africa: p48(t). Royal Botanic Gardens, Kew: pp34(t), 74(t). Rudolph Spanner: p75(t). Tobias Spanner: pp32(b), 59(t). Mick Turland: p63(t).

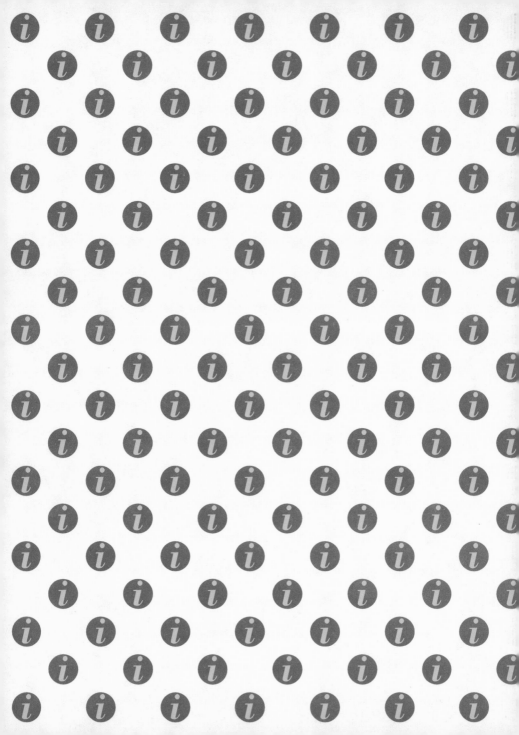

```
        BOOKS-A-MILLION #788
          9131 MIDLOTHIAN
               TURNPIKE
          RICHMOND    VA  23235
STORE #0788   REGISTER #  2
1 10 0840029909           3.98
2 10 0840029911           3.98
SUB TOTAL      :          7.96
SALES TAX  4.50%:          .36
TOTAL          :          8.32
AMOUNT TENDERED :        10.00
CHANGE DUE     :          1.68
  1  CASH            88
  13:39:20       3/09/95  SG
    THANK YOU FOR SHOPPING AT
         BOOKS-A-MILLION
    RICHMOND'S LARGEST BOOKSTORE
ASK ABOUT OUR MILLIONAIRE'S CLUB!!!
************************************
------------ JOIN OUR CLUB !! ------------
YOU WOULD HAVE SAVED TODAY        $.84
```

Love or
Loneliness...
You Decide

BOOKS BY DR. SCHULLER AVAILABLE IN THIS SPECIAL EDITION

Living Positively One Day at a Time
Love or Loneliness . . . You Decide
Reach Out for New Life
Your Future is Your Friend

Dr. Robert H. Schuller

Love or Loneliness... You Decide

The Cathedral Press
Garden Grove, California

Copyright © 1974, 1991 by Robert H. Schuller
All rights reserved under International and Pan-American
Copyright Conventions. No part of this book may be reproduced
in any form or by any electronic or mechanical means, including
information storage and retrieval systems, without permission
in writing from the publisher.

ISBN: 1-879989-03-4

Published by The Cathedral Press
Crystal Cathedral Ministries
13280 Chapman Avenue
Garden Grove, California 92640.
Distributed by Barbour and Company, Inc.
164 Mill Street
Westwood, New Jersey 07675

Text design by Wanda Pfloog
Set in ITC New Baskerville by Classic Typography

Printed in the United States of America

*This book is dedicated to the loyal staff and
faithful volunteers who help me in my ministry.
They are truly instruments of Christ's love,
healing the loneliness in the hearts of people*

To My New Readers

I am especially pleased that this book, along with several others, is again available. A number of members and friends of the Crystal Cathedral Ministries have indicated an interest in having them back in print and we are pleased that we were able to comply with their requests.

Since these books were first written and published, there have been many changes in the world and in our lives. Some of the wonderful people from whom I have learned are no longer with us. My children are now all grown and enrich our lives every day.

At first I thought I would revise these books but as our ministry continues to grow, finding the time to do so was almost impossible. Then I realized that revision wasn't really necessary—the references and illustrations are as valid as ever in calling our attentions to the everlasting Gospel. I hope you will find this book a life-enriching and life-changing experience.

Robert Schuller

Contents

Preface

RECENTLY, ONE OF our "Hour of Power" listeners, Abigail Van Buren, known to many of you as Dear Abby, was talking to me. We agreed that the bulk of our mail indicates that there are multiplied tens of millions of Americans who are desperate for acceptance, understanding and love.

People who are hungry for self-worth, and for acceptance by others, need an experience of authentic love. This powerful, helpful love is defined in the Bible in I Corinthians, Chapter 13.

I know of no other chapter in the Bible—unless it would be the 23rd Psalm—that has been so meaningful in revolutionizing human lives as this great chapter on love in the Holy Bible.

For several months I delivered messages on this chapter to my national television audience. The response was overwhelming. We have, accordingly, selected those messages that were in greatest demand and herewith offer them as a unity of hope—for you.

Here's a tremendous suggestion. Read this "greatest chapter in the Bible" once a day for a month. And see what a miracle you'll experience!

Yours in Christ's happy service!

Robert Schuller

I Corinthians, Chapter 13
Here is real love . . .

THOUGH I SPEAK with the tongues of men and of
angels, and have not charity, I am become as sound-
ing brass, or a tinkling cymbal.

2 And though I have the gift of prophecy, and understand all mysteries, and all knowledge; and though
I have all faith, so that I could remove mountains, and
have not charity, I am nothing.

3 And though I bestow all my goods to feed the poor,
and though I give my body to be burned, and have not
charity, it profiteth me nothing.

4 Charity suffereth long, and is kind; charity envieth
not; charity vaunteth not itself, is not puffed up,

5 Doth not behave itself unseemly, seeketh not her own, is not easily provoked, thinketh no evil;

6 Rejoiceth not in iniquity, but rejoiceth in the truth;

7 Beareth all things, believeth all things, hopeth all things, endureth all things.

8 Charity never faileth: but whether there be prophecies, they shall fail; whether there be tongues, they shall cease; whether there be knowledge, it shall vanish away.

9 For we know in part, and we prophesy in part.

10 But when that which is perfect is come, then that which is in part shall be done away.

11 When I was a child, I spake as a child, I understood as a child, I thought as a child: but when I became a man, I put away childish things.

12 For now we see through a glass, darkly; but then face to face: now I know in part; but then shall I know even as also I am known.

13 And now abideth faith, hope, charity, these three; but the greatest of these is charity.

KING JAMES TRANSLATION

IF I SPEAK in the tongues of men and of angels, but I have not love, I am a noisy gong or a clanging cymbal. ²And if I have prophetic powers, and understand all mysteries and all knowledge, and if I have all faith, so as to remove mountains, but have not love, I am nothing. ³If I give away all I have, and if I deliver my body to be burned, but have not love, I gain nothing. ⁴Love is patient and kind; love is not jealous or boastful; ⁵it is not arrogant or rude. Love does not insist on its own way; it is not irritable or resentful; ⁶it does not rejoice at wrong, but rejoices in the right. ⁷Love bears all things, believes all things, hopes all things, endures all things. ⁸Love never ends; as for prophecies, they will pass away; as for tongues, they will cease; as for knowledge, it will pass away. ⁹For our knowledge is imperfect and our prophecy is imperfect; ¹⁰but when the perfect comes, the imperfect will pass away. ¹¹When I was a child, I spoke like a child, I thought like a child, I reasoned like a child; when I became a man, I gave up childish ways. ¹²For now we see in a mirror dimly, but then face to face. Now I know in part; then I shall understand fully, even as I have been fully understood. ¹³So faith, hope, love abide, these three; but the greatest of these is love.

REVISED STANDARD TRANSLATION

IF I SPEAK with the eloquence of men and of angels, but have no love, I become no more than blaring brass or crashing cymbal. If I have the gift of foretelling the future and hold in my mind not only all human knowledge but the very secrets of God, and if I have that absolute faith which can move mountains, but have no love, I amount to nothing at all. If I dispose of all that I possess, yes, even if I give my own body to be burned, but have no love, I achieve precisely nothing.

This love of which I speak is slow to lose patience — it looks for a way of being constructive. It is not possessive: it is neither anxious to impress nor does it cherish inflated ideas of its own importance.

Love has good manners and does not pursue selfish advantage. It is not touchy. It does not keep account of evil or gloat over the wickedness of other people. On the contrary, it is glad with all good men when truth prevails.

Love knows no limit to its endurance, no end to its trust, no fading of its hope; it can outlast anything. It is, in fact, the one thing that still stands when all else has fallen.

For if there are prophecies they will be fulfilled and done with, if there are "tongues" the need for them will disappear, if there is knowledge it will be swallowed up in truth. For our knowledge is always incomplete and our prophecy is always incomplete, and when the complete comes, that is the end of the incomplete.

When I was a little child I talked and felt and thought like a little child. Now that I am a man my childish speech and feeling and thought have no further significance for me.

At present we are men looking at puzzling reflections in a mirror. The time will come when we shall see reality whole and face to face! At present all I know is a little fraction of the truth, but the time will come when I shall know it as fully as God now knows me!

In this life we have three great lasting qualities— faith, hope and love. But the greatest of them is love.

PHILLIPS TRANSLATION

I F I HAD THE GIFT of being able to speak in other languages without learning them, and could speak in every language there is in all of heaven and earth, but didn't love others, I would only be making noise.

2 If I had the gift of prophecy and knew all about what is going to happen in the future, knew everything about everything, but didn't love others, what good would it do? Even if I had the gift of faith so that I could speak to a mountain and make it move, I would still be worth nothing at all without love.

3 If I gave everything I have to poor people, and if I were burned alive for preaching the Gospel but didn't love others, it would be of no value whatever.

4 Love is very patient and kind, never jealous or envious, never boastful or proud.

5 Never haughty or selfish or rude. Love does not demand its own way. It is not irritable or touchy. It does not hold grudges and will hardly even notice when others do it wrong.

6 It is never glad about injustice, but rejoices whenever truth wins out.

7 If you love someone you will be loyal to him no matter what the cost. You will always believe in him, always expect the best of him, and always stand your ground in defending him.

8 All the special gifts and powers from God will someday come to an end, but love goes on forever. Someday prophecy, and speaking unknown languages, and special knowledge—these gifts will disappear.

9 Now we know so little, even with our special gifts, and the preaching of those most gifted is still so poor.

10 But when we have been made perfect and complete, then the need for these inadequate special gifts will come to an end, and they will disappear.

11 It's like this: when I was a child I spoke and thought and reasoned as a child does. But when I became a man my thoughts grew far beyond those of my childhood, and now I have put away the childish things.

12 In the same way, we can see and understand only a little about God now, as if we were peering at His reflection in a poor mirror; but someday we are going to see Him in His completeness, face to face. Now all that I know is hazy and blurred, but then I will see everything clearly, just as clearly as God sees into my heart right now.

13 There are three things that remain—faith, hope, and love—and the greatest of these is love.

LIVING TRANSLATION

·1·

Love Is The Greatest

" . . . but the greatest of these is love."
I COR. 13:13

No problem is too big
for God's power;
No person is too small
for God's love.

I F THERE IS ONE thing that is sure and certain, it is
that nothing is sure and certain." That, at least, is what
the cynic would say. The cynic would tell us that change
and decay are all around us and that this is the one and
only certainty. And, of course, that is the great para-
dox. If the only thing that is certain is change, then
nothing is certain.

Well, the good news I have for you is this: *There is
something that does not change!* And that something is
man—you and me and every man. Everybody who is
born, everybody who lives and everybody who dies,
every human being all around the world is the same,

and he doesn't change. His basic needs do not change. Every human being who is born needs to eat, breathe and drink water, or he will die. The body does not change in its demands. And the heart of man does not change. Every heart needs the food of human love.

What is that deep yearning in your heart? Are there times when your heart almost seems moist in its crying out for nourishment? What is it that you need deep down in your soul?

Have you felt a restlessness within your heart? You know what it's like to feel hungry. The stomach seems empty and it craves and calls for food. Have you had something like that as far as your heart is concerned? Psychologists call it, of course, being emotionally deprived. We use the words *heart hunger*.

The heart has a constant hunger for love. Nothing else satisfies. It's like going to a refrigerator and opening it and wondering what you're hungry for. You see this and you see that, and you finally take a nibble and go to bed still unsatisfied, not knowing what you really wanted. That hungry, craving restlessness—your heart has it. It's really a mark of health. A body that doesn't have a physical appetite is sick. And if you don't have that constant recurring restlessness of a hunger in your heart, then you're not healthy. That recurring restlessness of the heart's hunger is a heart's call for the food of love.

Long before this youthful science called Psychiatry, there was a book, a book called the Bible. And it said, man's body needs food and drink, and man's heart needs love. And if it does not have love, that heart will

14

be undernourished. It will cry out for nutrition. How it cries out — you know. Look around you at the world!

The good news I have for you is that you do not change, I do not change, the Bible does not change and God does not change. Your heart needs love and God is able to give it to you. And God has set things up in such a way that you can get it.

Recently Mrs. Schuller and I and my two little girls spent a few days at a mountain cabin we have high up in the California mountains, a place we built many, many years ago when things were still cheap! My littlest girl came to me one morning and said, "Daddy, in our Daily Vacation Bible School we were taught that if you take a pine cone and put peanut butter on it and you sprinkle bird seed on it, the bird seed will stick to the peanut butter, and you can put the pine cone out and little birds will eat the seed from the pine cone."

I said to her, "You don't have to go through all that rigmarole. We've got some bird seed up in the cabin. Just put it right on the deck, and the birds will come up and eat it. You don't need to put it on peanut butter and on a pine cone and all of that."

I gave her some bird seed, she put it on the railing of our deck, and sure enough, the bluejays came and gobbled it down, and the squirrels came and they gobbled it down. The jays fought with the squirrels and they all fought with each other, but they all got a stomach full.

"I still think it would be nice to put it on a pine cone," my daughter persisted. It sounded like a nice project, so I finally gave in.

We went for a walk in the woods, and under one of the great old trees in the forest we found some pine cones and took them home. I tied a rope on the very top little prong of the cone so that I could tie it on the branch of a tree. Then we got out the peanut butter. What a mess trying to get peanut butter on and inside all of these little prongs! Then she sprinkled the bird seed on it, and sure enough, all the bird seed that hit the peanut butter struck. But what didn't hit the peanut butter didn't stick, and it rolled like miniature marbles all over the decking where it crunched under our shoes for days later.

Finally she got it all speckled with bird seed. We took it outdoors and she tied it on a branch, right on the tip, so it hung down draping the branch, like a too-heavy ornament on the tender tip of a Christmas tree.

"Gretchen," I said, "you should tie it in the solid middle."

"No," she said, "I'll tie it here at the end."

So she left it hanging at the end. Pretty soon the blue-jays came, but they just flew around and didn't dare to land on the pine cone, because it was weaving back and forth and looked too unsteady for them; they didn't dare to sit on it. They stood on the branch, but they couldn't begin to get at it. They flew away in disgust.

Pretty soon the squirrels came. They had smelled the peanut butter. Up the tree they went and onto the branch. I can still see one squirrel running down that branch, and as he's getting closer to the end, the branch starts to bend. He's just about to the spot where the rope is tied when the branch bends way down, and he backs off fearfully down the tree. What a lesson in frustration! He went up another branch, trying to approach it from the other way, but he was two feet away from it there. He ran down the railing and stuck his nose at it from there, but he was four feet away from it. Finally, in frustration, he ran off.

"Gretchen," I said, "it is a sublime failure. They can't eat it."

And then it happened. All the *little* birds started coming. They came and literally walked down the rope and nibbled the food from the top so they wouldn't get their feet dirty with peanut butter. An amazing sight! Then more little birds came. One very resourceful "possibility thinking" winged creature grabbed the bottom of the pine cone where there was no peanut butter and he nibbled from the bottom. So the little birds had their feast, and the big bully bluejay and the big bully grey squirrel were left unfed. (But they didn't need it!)

Now what's the good news? Some of you people are poor. And you look at the very, very wealthy and you say, "God is unfair. They get it all, and I'm left with empty hands." The good news I have for you is this: As far as the food for your heart is concerned, God has set things up in such a way that the little people can always get what they need. The pine cone is set up so that the little birds are sure that they get what they need. And God has set this world in such a way that the little people can always get the love their hearts hunger for. We used this saying on our "Hour of Power" calendar one year:

No problem is too big
for God's power;
No person is too small
for God's love.

God loves you. And God is willing to fill your heart with that deep love. Love, the deepest need, is all over the world.

A while back a member of my staff calculated that I am a million miler. "What does that mean?" I asked.

And he said, "You have flown over a million miles in your life." It sounded like an awful lot.

"I think you're exaggerating," I told him. But he proved that it was not incorrect. I began thinking about it as I studied this chapter on Love. I really have travelled a lot.

I have touched the grease-covered naked bodies of people some would call savages in the highlands of New Guinea, and deep in their expressive eyes I saw the same thing I see when I look into your eyes—love.

And then I remember the bronzed, tan skin of the beautiful people who live in Shinaigar in the cool shadows of the Himalayas, not far from Nepal. There, living in their houseboats in the cool, high mountain lake are some of the most beautiful people in the world. Again, by our standards, poor and illiterate, uncultured, but what is culture without love?

St. Paul says in I Corinthians 13, if I'm eloquent and have the gift of tongues and do not have love, what good is eloquence? If I have oratorical ability, and do not have authentic love, it's nothing but a big show. If I have faith so that I can move mountains, but if I do not have love, then you'd better watch out, for faith without love is the most dangerous thing in the world.

One summer I was with a tour of eighty "Hour of Power" people. I want to say that it was one of the most enjoyable experiences of my life for this reason (and this is a testimony): I've never been more excited than I am today, but I do not love my work more than I did the first three years that I was the pastor of my church, and I'll tell you why. I love people. I thrive on people. During the first three years after Mrs. Schuller and I started this church, I knew all the members by name, and I didn't have to think when I saw someone coming. I didn't have to get tense inside and say, "Oh, what's his name, I can't remember it!" (Now I sometimes suffer from guilt and tension and miserable feelings because I can't remember everyone's name.)

I love people. This church is big. God has called me to a larger ministry and I can't know everybody's name, and I miss that more than you will ever know. So when we planned that "Hour of Power" tour, we said we were going to limit it to eighty people. I had a reason for that. I was going to be on that tour, and I wanted to have only a small group so that I would know everybody's name. I was thrilled, because in twenty-four hours I knew everybody's name. So I was able to love every person personally!

Some years ago there was a musical on Broadway about a little girl who came down from the hills of Italy to join the circus. She said goodbye to her tiny hometown called Mira. Lonesome, homesick, wandering through the quiet carnival tents, she started to sing this song: "What I like of Mira, is everybody knows my name. Yes, everybody knows my name. Now what do you think of that? Now what do you think of that? Yes, everybody knows my name."

I know that feeling. I was born in a town called Alton, Iowa. It was huge, I thought; it had 400 people. And I went to high school in Newkirk, Iowa. The total population of the high school was 73 when I was there. Our senior class had 14, which broke a record, the largest class in the history of Newkirk High School. They graduated me, and now they're out of business! They no longer exist!

Well, on that tour I knew everybody's name. And I can tell you their stories. I found out that *everybody had a dream, and everybody had a hurt.* There were two beautiful girls. Their brother had been murdered some years ago. But they knew they'd find an even more beautiful faith than they already had when they went back to the Holy Land, and they did. There was another woman, a lovely woman. Her husband had died many years ago, leaving her with little children. Everybody has a hurt. Everybody has a dream. Everybody needs to be loved. And I've never been happier than I was on that tour because with me were eighty people that I was able to know and meet and love. That's a great, great feeling, it really is!

Love. You need it. I need it. Everybody, all over the world, needs it.

Russia, as you know, has tried to educate man into being a cold, calculating, intellectualized, rationalized creature, so that he's basically a computer that responds to the guy who pushes a button. Communism basically says that man, the emotional creature, is weak. It is at this doctrine of man that Communism and Christianity are totally irreconcilable, because Communism says that man is basically a rational creature, and Christianity says that man is basically an emotional creature.

I subscribe to a couple of wire services. Several years ago this report came over one of them:

"Communist China has denounced the Kremlin leaders for allowing religious fever to grip the Soviet Union. Peking radio, in a recent broadcast, said that a religious fever is spreading across the Communist Soviet Union. Describing what is called 'an upsurge in religious practice in the Soviet Union,' the Chinese broadcoast continued, '. . . tens of thousands of religious believers swarmed into the churches this past Easter. There they ate wafers, they made crosses and sang hymns to celebrate the resurrection of Jesus. Moscow's 54 churches, guarded by police and militant groups, were jammed packed. Why has such a phenomenon of such social retrogression appeared in a so-called developed socialist country, in the land of the great Lenin?'" the broadcast asked rhetorically. Well, we know the answer.

One summer I went through Zurich, and I thought of Solzhenitzyn who was living there. Solzhenitzyn — *think of it, the number one poet in the Soviet Union* — product of its educational systems, product of its indoctrination, product of its scientific materialism, product of its dialectical materialism, always protected from Western influence, now has come out and made this statement:

"I myself see Christianity as the only living spiritual force capable of healing my land." It's incredible! Even a totally repressive society based on total control is not able to change man's deep heart hunger for love.

What is that love that satisfies? It is only Christ. It is only God. That's what it is!

Now the good news I have, and it applies to every person, no matter who you are, is that God has set things up in such a way that He is able to provide love to your hungry heart. Even though you may think you're a very, very little person, *He knows you.* And He'll take care of your heart's hunger for love.

I had breakfast one morning at a little restaurant in the Beau Rivage Hotel, in Lausanne, Switzerland, and talked with Malcolm Muggeridge. You may not know the name, but Malcolm Muggeridge was once probably the most recognized face and name in England. A poll conducted in London at the time asked, "What face would you recognize first on the street?" Malcolm Muggeridge was No. 1; the Queen of England was No. 2. Now that's how famous he was! Some of you may remember his monthly column in a leading American magazine. Some of you may remember him as the editor of *Punch* magazine. He had an interesting life. As a young man he was a radical socialist. He thought that socialism, as an economic system, would solve all the human problems and we'd have a perfect society. From that he moved on into agnosticism, and then he became an atheist. Then he was fascinated by communism. So as a journalist he requested an assignment to the Soviet Union and was given it. He spent years there, only to discover to his chagrin that it was a repressive society, that it didn't satisfy; it just didn't have the answers.

Once he was on a journalism assignment in India. In Calcutta he met a diminutive woman by the name of Mother Theresa, a Roman Catholic nun. Now there are loads of people in this world who are on the edge of sainthood. They're such beautiful Christians, but nobody comes closer to being called a saint and earning it than Mother Theresa. She took the dying people from the streets of Calcutta, touched them, loved them and kissed them so that as they were dying they would know that somebody loved them while they were leaving the earth. Incredible!

Muggeridge saw in her a love that you cannot explain by psychology, any science or by any anthropological principles. You cannot explain it from a sociological, a political or economic standpoint. There's only one way to explain it: *Something* has gripped that woman! "It" is Christ.

Well, it caused Muggeridge to start reading his Bible. To make a long story short, he became a Christian. As he has said, "Hedonism, as a philosophy, can be very appealing for those who can stand it and those who can afford it. After all, the lusts of life can be very, very delightful. The earth's smells and sounds can be very sweet. Sexual love can bring its golden hours, but, in the end, it does not satisfy.

"Still there was something in my heart that was hungry. Now that I look back on it, it is as if I were all my life in a dungeon where both of my hands were manacled, and around me were crowds of people with their manacled hands in the same dungeon. Fantasies and furies were around me. In my fantasies there was no God, no heaven, no hell, no sin and no Saviour. Yes, I felt manacled. One manacle was the desires of my body and flesh and my lust; the other manacle my will and its driving me to do and to be. Then suddenly a couple of years ago I looked up and in my dungeon I saw a light, a window in the top and light coming out. Above it, I suspected, a whole heaven! The heaven was God! The window was Jesus Christ! The ray that shone down on me was the Holy Spirit! And love came to me, love such as I have never known, and it was beautiful."

It can happen to you. If you're in a dungeon and you feel manacled, look up! Find love!

LOVE . . . it is the greatest!

·2·

Love — The Force That Puts Power In Your Faith

"Love believes all things."
I COR. 13:7

I love Christ too much
to ever doubt God!

FOR YEARS I'VE read I Corinthians 13 with what I now view to be a distorted impression. I've always thought that Paul was really holding up three lovelies in a beauty contest. One was Faith, one was Hope and one was Love. And when the final contest was completed, Love won the crown. Faith was the first runnerup, and Hope came in third. In other words, I had the impression that Paul was putting Faith and Love and Hope *in competition* with each other. Now that's not a true interpretation at all. The insight I have now, and I'm excited to share it with you, is that what Paul is simply saying is that the three are a Holy Trinity. Love is what wraps them all together. The truth is, love is a mighty faith-building power. *"Love believes all things."* (I Cor. 13:7.)

So, I Corinthians Chapter 13 is not a putdown of faith. You've got to believe, you know. Blake put it this way:

Life's dim windows of the soul
Distort the heavens from pole to pole.
And makes us to believe a lie
When we see with and not through the eye.

We need faith. The truth is, love is impossible without faith, and faith is unacceptable without love. Think of that: *Love is impossible without faith.*

I've been married for twenty-five years to my first and only wife, and if you ask me what is love, I would say first of all, it is *respect;* secondly, it is *faith.*

I am thinking of a man who is unmarried. He is in his fifties. He was despairing before me recently because his life is lonely; he has never had a family.

"The trouble is," he said, "I once knew a young girl, but there wasn't the passion for her that I thought should have been there, so I foolishly thought I didn't love her. However, I deeply respected and trusted her! Now, in retrospect, I see that this was love, but I didn't know it! And I let it pass me by."

Today I call upon you to build your faith around a heart of love. Have you seen people who have faith which seems to move mountains? And other people who profess faith in God and in Jesus Christ, but nothing miraculous or joyful seems to be happening in their lives? Now what's the difference? The difference probably is that the one person has a faith with a heart of love. And the other person has a faith but love is not at the heart of it! That's what Paul is talking about here. So what I'm saying is that love is the power-center behind a mountain-moving faith.

When love is at the core of your faith, it puts five miracle-working powers into your belief.

1. *Love puts renewing power in faith.* When love is so strong it won't allow you to doubt for long, then it puts power at the center of your faith. Some people say to me, "Dr. Schuller, where do you get your faith?" And I think the answer is simple:

> *I love Christ too much*
> *to ever doubt God!*

If at the core of your faith there is love—for your work, for your project, for your dream, for your cause, for your husband, for your wife—when love is at the power-core of faith, then faith will never quit. It will come back, it will start over, it will try again. You will reorganize, you will reschedule, you will reexamine, you will rededicate, but you do not resign. The kind of faith that never quits, the kind of faith that is constantly renewed, is faith that has love at the center. Faith and love are twins. Love puts renewing power in faith. Then what happens?

2. *Love puts realigning power in faith.* What do I mean? I mean when love is in the core of your faith, you con-

stantly realign your faith to make sure that your faith is focusing on service and not on yourself. And that's crucial.

I recently had to have my tires realigned. I got new tires four months ago and I haven't put many miles on them, but suddenly I looked at them the other day and I noticed they were completely worn on one side. And what was worse, I could hardly drive down the freeway without almost jiggling apart. It was absolutely uncontrollable to drive. So I had my front wheels realigned.

And you and I must do this with our faith constantly. Realign your faith to make sure that your faith is focused on service and not on yourself.

I recently received a letter from one of the Presbyterian pastors who was here for our last Institute for Successful Church Leadership. In it he wrote, "You know, that Institute changed my life. When I was a young man and had just entered the ministry, I really had my eyes on Christ, and it was beautiful. Somewhere along the line I got my eyes off Him and I became ambitious. My eyes were on professional pursuits and on my career. When Dr. Schuller shared how real Jesus Christ was to him, He became real to me again. My life has been changed." He's been realigned, you see. Love at the power-center of your faith will cause you to refocus on service and not on self. Love at the power-center, then, gives constant renewing power, constant realigning power, and obviously what follows then is that you get restraining power on your faith.

3. *Love puts restraining power on faith.* Power to keep your faith from running over people just to get what you want. Remember, love without faith is impossible; and faith without love is totally unacceptable. It's downright damaging.

A businessman said to me once after I had finished one of my lectures at a sales conference, "I've got a problem. You know, I really think that I could expand my business to really cover the whole country, but if I did it I would put a lot of little guys out of business. As a Christian I don't think I should do that, do you?"

I answered, "I don't think so either."

4. *Love puts a redeeming power in faith.* When there is love at the power-center of your faith, there is a renewing power, a realigning power, and a restraining power. Naturally, then, your faith becomes a redeeming power. Instead of hurting people, you help people. Instead of being a destroyer, you become a builder. Instead of just being a teacher, trying to draw your maximum salary and maximum benefits, you're primarily concerned about these kids and how you can build a person. And as a doctor you're not primarily concerned about how many fees you can attract, but about how you can be a physician who heals the whole person. And as a businessman you're primarily concerned not about profit margins, you must concern yourself with that, but you're constantly concerned about serving people who have needs that must be met. And as a lawyer, you look upon yourself as a counselor to help people and to advise

them. And as a laboring man or a deliveryman, you really want to help people. You care about them.

A couple of weeks ago, when we spent a few days at our mountain cabin, it was necessary for me to order two deliveries to our place. Both deliveries really shocked me. The first item came in a heavy carton. The man drove his truck up and put it at the front door. I was about to say goodbye when he said, "It's kind of heavy. Where would you like it? Can't I carry it in for you?"

I said, "Well, yes, thank you." And so he brought it in the house.

"Be glad to carry it upstairs for you," he continued. I was amazed. Then he cut the carton open, which kind of shocked me, and said, "Let's make sure all the pieces are here before I leave. It would be too bad if I got home and you found a couple of pieces missing." (I've had that happen. Haven't you?)

He took the thing out, checked all the pieces, and they were all there. Then he picked up all the pieces of paper, stuffed them in the box and asked, "Do you want the box or shall I take it along for you?"

I said, "That would be fine."

And then he saw some little mess that he had made from some of this stuff and said, "Do you have a broom?"

I got out a broom and a pan and he swept it up. I couldn't believe it.

He looked at me and said, "Haven't I met you some place? You sure look familiar."

"Do you ever watch religious television programs?" I asked.

His face glowed as he answered, "Oh, you're Dr. Schuller. I didn't recognize you in your swimming suit!" He then really opened up. "Isn't this business of being a Christian wonderful?" He was full of the Spirit of Christ.

And I said, "It sure makes a difference in people, when it turns you into the kind of deliveryman you are. That's great."

Only a few days after that I had another delivery, and it was the same kind of story. The guy couldn't do enough to be helpful. As he was leaving, he said he thought he recognized me. Then he told me, "Oh, we've enjoyed the 'Hour of Power.' In fact, I'm a committed Christian, and I'm going to be a minister. I just don't have enough education yet to have a church of my own. But I'm going to go into full-time ministry of the Lord, and thank you for what you've done in my life."

Faith is constantly *renewed* if love is at the core.
Faith is constantly *realigned* if love is at the core.
Faith is constantly *restrained* if love is at the core.
Faith is constantly *redeemed* if love is at the core.

No wonder, then, that faith is constantly *rejoicing* if love is at the core. And that's what makes faith a mountain-moving power, because the rejoicing keeps you so energetic, so joyful, so happy.

5. *Love puts rejoicing power in your faith.* What good is faith if it will die, or if it's damaging, or if it leads to despair? Your faith does not need to be that way. It can rejoice!

We all know people who have a lot of positive thinking and possibility thinking. They make their goals, they
achieve success, they even become very wealthy and
sometimes very powerful and end up dying from an
overdose. What good is that?

Love without faith is impossible, and faith without
love is totally unacceptable. All the possibility thinking in the world is dangerous unless Jesus Christ, through
the Holy Spirit, has control over your heart and fills
you with His love. If that happens, you will be happy
in your success because you will be so helpful.

I was preaching in New Jersey, and there was a line of
people who met me afterwards. In the line was one
young man who said, "I'm a Presbyterian pastor, and
I made this trip which took me a couple of hundred
miles to drive here to meet you, Dr. Schuller. I'm so
glad you agreed to meet people afterwards, because I've
come bearing a message. One of the leading members
of my church, who was in her late forties, died some-
time ago from cancer. The last year she was unable to
come out to church at all. Every Sunday she watched
television, the 'Hour of Power,' in her New Jersey bed-
room. Shortly before she passed away she said to me,
'Reverend, if you ever get a chance to meet anybody
from that Hour of Power or Dr. Schuller, please go and
bring him this message from me. Tell him that because
of his ministry, I didn't spend the last year of my life
dying from cancer, I spent the last year of my life *living*
with cancer.'"

Do you see why I'm happy? When Christ is in the center of your life, then love is at the center of your faith! Your faith is constantly renewed; it does not die. It's constantly realigned; it's not distracted. It's constantly restrained, never demeaning.

It's constantly redeeming, never destructive. So it's constantly rejoicing, never despairing.

·3·

Compromise
Can Be Kingly

"Love seeketh not her own."
I COR. 13:5

No man has a right
to demand
all of his rights
all of the time!

ONE OF THE REVISED VERSIONS translates the phrase "Love seeketh not her own" this way:

"Love does not demand its own way."

I suggest that this brings us to the thought that compromise can be kingly. We all have been warned from childhood never to compromise. And indeed it is a truth that there are principles that you must never compromise. Remember Tevye, the father hero in *Fiddler on the Roof*? He had that surprisingly marvelous balance in the realm of compromising. He had the ability to

see both sides when he said, " . . . on the other hand . . . "
But he reaches one point when he says, "There is no
other hand!" There is a point beyond which you cannot compromise.

All of which leads us to probably one of the most
important questions we have to ask as Christians, and
that is, "When do we compromise and when don't we?"

Have you noticed that love, for some people, is very
wishy-washy, while love, for others, seems to be strong
as steel? The people whose love is strong as steel are
people for whom self-denial is at the core of their love.
For what is compromising? It is self-denial. Compromising is lowering yourself only to be lifted.

Two boys were trying to play on a hobby horse outside of a department store where you put in a dime
and the horse goes up and down. They were both trying to ride at the same time when one boy said, "You
know, if both of us didn't try to get on at the same time,
I could have a much better ride."

Compromising is *lowering yourself* to give someone else
an opportunity.

Compromising is *looking;* looking for better ideas,
new insights, broader views, brighter ways to help. It
assumes that somebody else knows something you don't
know.

Compromising is *listening:* It's listening to what others
are saying. It's listening to what others are demanding.
It's listening to what others claim are their rights. It's
listening to what others hold as their opinions, their
views and their interpretations of the Bible, even when
you don't agree.

We've reached a point in our world and in our country where without compromising we're all going to be bruised over the same hobby horse, and nobody is going to have a decent ride.

Compromising is looking, listening, lowering and *living with the spirit of community.* A give-and-take attitude. If you forget everything else I write in this book, don't forget this next sentence:

> *No man has a right to*
> *demand all of his rights*
> *all of the time.*

"I know my rights," you say. No man has a right to demand all of his rights all of the time, if he wants to be a part of a community. So what's compromising? It's looking for better ideas, broader views. It's listening to what others are saying, thinking and interpreting. And it's living with them, even when you don't share their viewpoint.

Compromising is *learning how to live abundantly,* even when you don't get your way. And it's learning how to be happy and pleasant, instead of being a baby and pouting just because things don't go the way you want them to go. That's what compromise is. It's looking, it's listening, it's living, it's learning, and it's summed up in two words: *Letting go!*

Yes, *compromising is letting God have His way and His will in your life.* That probably will be what you really do not want to do! But that's the difference between being moral or immoral. An immoral person is some-

41

body who does what he wants to do, when he wants to do it, the way he wants to do it, whether it is right or not. That's immorality. By contrast, morality is doing what is right, even if you don't like it.

Compromise can be kingly then, can't it?! When you look for better ideas, when you listen to what others are saying and thinking, when you live with the spirit of community and begin to learn how to live happily even when your man isn't elected to office, and when you learn then to let go and lower yourself and let God take over, can't you see this is when compromise is kingly?

So when do you compromise? That's the question. I want to suggest four times when compromising will make a peasant into a king:

1. *Compromise in the face of a hurt that you can do nothing about.* My friend Pat Shaughnessy is the pastor of a church in Phoenix, Arizona. His church was not moving and he wasn't able to come to the Institute at the time it was in session, so he got a copy of my book, *Move Ahead with Possibility Thinking.* As he's told many people, it transformed his life and it transformed his church which is suddenly blossoming and growing. Right now they're building a million dollar church to handle the bulging congregation.

I tell him, "God spoke to you through the book, Pat, and I thank Him for that. I prayed for that. Give credit where credit is due. It's God who did it."

"Yes, you're right," he said.

Some years ago I returned from Europe to find a memo for me to call Pat at a Los Angeles hospital.

"What are you doing there?" I asked.

And he said, "Let me tell you what happened. I was on my way to Korea a few weeks ago, standing at the Pan Am air counter, when all of a sudden there was an explosion. Three people were killed. I was closest to the bomb, and suddenly I found myself lying on the floor. My right leg was blown off between the hip and the knee. Blood just gushed out. But I never lost consciousness.

"My first thought was, 'Lord, if I have to go, I'm ready. But I don't want to. I enjoy preaching about Jesus so much because Christ is such a wonderful person.'

"My second thought was of my wife. I hoped she would not be too hurt by what was happening to me.

"Then on the way to the hospital they were pumping blood into me, and it was a mad scene. They said I wouldn't live, and I was wide awake. Then this thought struck me, 'I don't need a right leg to preach the gospel!'"

Pat has compromised. He has accepted the loss of a leg. Look at what you have left, not at what you have lost. You must compromise in the face of a hurt or a loss that you cannot change.

2. *Compromise in the face of humility.* I recall an incident in the life of Schweitzer, that great dedicated man who had over fifty honorary doctorate degrees. Albert Schweitzer has to be one of the greatest men of our century. He built his hospital in Africa, in the Belgian

Congo. The natives normally would do anything for him. But one day when he needed wood hauled to build a wall, he asked one tribal native to carry some wood. The native, who had learned to read and was busy reading a book, said, "I am an intellectual and I do not carry wood."

Schweitzer, in the face of that, looked at him and said, "Well, I congratulate you. I always wanted to be an intellectual, but I never succeeded, so I'll carry the wood." And he did!

3. *Compromise in the face of helpfulness.* I recall an incident in the life of Abraham Lincoln. At the height of the Civil War, he wondered how the battle was going. Rather than call General McClellan to come to him at the White House and report, he decided that he and the secretary of war would go out to the general's house in the battle area.

They made their way to the general's home and waited. Finally the general came in, walked right on upstairs to his room and never acknowledged the president. They thought he'd be back in a minute with cleaner garb, but he didn't come back. They asked the maid to go upstairs, but when she came down she was aghast!

"I'm sorry, Mr. President," she said, "but he said to me, 'Tell the president I'm tired and that I've gone to bed.'"

The secretary of war said, "Surely you're not going to let him get by with that. You will relieve him, will you not?"

44

The president thought about it for a long time, and finally when he broke the silence he said, "No, I will not relieve him. That man wins battles, and I would hold his horse and clean his shoes if it would hasten the end of this bloodshed by one hour."

Doesn't that remind you of our Lord Jesus Christ? He overheard His followers talking behind his back. "When Jesus is gone, who is going to be the top man here? You, Peter? You, John, or Luke?"

Do you know what Jesus did? He asked for a basin of water and He asked for a towel. And before they had their communion He got down and started to wash their feet.

Peter said, "Wait a minute, I should wash your feet. You shouldn't wash mine."

But He just moved from foot to foot and washed their dirty feet and wiped them with a towel.

You compromise if you can teach somebody a lesson by doing it, indeed you do. Schweitzer hauled wood. Lincoln would hold the man's horse. Jesus washed the disciples' feet. Great men have become kings by learning when to bow, when to compromise.

4. *Compromise in the face of holiness.* Don't you sense it, that there is a God and that He has a plan for your life? Don't you feel it, that there's a road that He wants you to walk on?

Some of you are running so fast. But what's the use of running so fast if you're on the wrong road? I would add, I see what some of you people are holding on to in life. For some it may be status, for others dollars, and others things. All of which some day will have to slip out of your hand. And when your life is finished they will mean nothing to you. I would ask you this question, *"What's the use of holding on to something that isn't tied down to anything?"*

Once God came to this world in the form of a man, and He died on the cross to prove to you that He loves you so much that He would stop at nothing to save you. And to gain power out of that cross, even eternal life, you must compromise your will to God's will. Say, "Father, not my will but Thine be done." *There is no conversion without compromise!*

You know, in old England when someone was to be knighted, the queen or the king tapped each shoulder of that person with a sword, and he was declared to be a knight. But there's one thing they had to do in order to become a knight. They had to be humble; they had to kneel; they had to bow; they had to compromise their pride. *They had to kneel to be knighted.*

I invite you now, whoever you are, to compromise what probably for you may be your pride, your greed, or maybe it's stubbornness, self-pity, jealousy, bitterness or your lust for something that is a sin that will keep God's Holy Spirit out of your life.

I suggest that you remember these words: *"Love does not demand its own way."* Love knows when you should give in and give up.

Let go and let God take over!

46

·4·

Living Beyond the Possibility of Personal Failure

"Love never fails."
I COR. 13:8

A beautiful person
is always a successful person.
And any person
can be beautiful!
So anyone can live
beyond failure.

MY TEXT NOW is from verse 8 of I Corinthians, Chapter 13, *"Love never fails."* I would say, you can love and lose, but you cannot love and fail. You can love and lose your life, (as happened to Jesus Christ on the cross), but you cannot fail as a person when you really love people sincerely.

Every human being can live beyond the possibility of personal failure. Everyone can be a success if he can learn to love. And that's all-important! For I don't suppose anything is more important than the consciousness that you, as a person, are a success and not a failure.

49

I remember so vividly a telephone call I received. It was from a woman calling from the midwest. She said, "Dr. Schuller, I am in my mid-fifties, and I'm finished with my life."

I told her that was a very negative attitude, but she continued, "But you don't know my life. I was a failure in high school. And I failed to go to college. I was a failure in my first marriage. My kids haven't turned out right, and I feel I'm a failure as a mother. I'm a failure as a wife. I never had a good job. My life has been one big fat failure. I'm not going to keep going."

And I'll tell you, my eyes were moist. How do you keep from crying when you come right down to a heart that is cracked and broken?

Nothing is more damning to the human spirit and to your mental health than if you ever get the idea that you have been a big failure. Success is a necessity.

W. Somerset Maugham said, "There's a common idea that success spoils people by making them vain and egotistical, but the truth is, this is erroneous and on the contrary, it makes people, for the most part, humble and tolerant and gentle. It is failure that makes people bitter and cruel. You need to feel that you are successful."

I'll never forget an article I read in the 1970s by Dr. Bertram Brown, the Director of the National Institute for Mental Health. In it he discussed one of our country's major problems, mental depression, and he listed this phenomenal statistic: Mental depression costs the United States $5 billion a year; that's in direct hospital-drugs expense which does not include the indirect cost of depression in forms of the funerals of the suicide victims. This does not include the expense to the tax-payers of people who are in mental hospitals, supported by your taxes, because they are depressed. The *direct,* immediate expense is $5 billion a year! Dr. Brown said, "Suicide today is the third cause of death among teen-agers and the eleventh cause among Americans in general."

Dr. Brown was asked the question, "Is there anything a depressive person can do for himself, short of seeking psychiatric help?"

The doctor's answer was, "Yes. Build into yourself the idea that you are not helpless and you are not hope-less."*

Then another question was addressed to him, "But how can you build into a person the feeling that he is not helpless and his life is not hopeless?"

He answered, "Give them success experiences to counteract feelings of helplessness."

That's where it comes out, and I hope that in some small measure what I say here will help to give you the key to success so that you will not feel helpless in the face of life and so that you will not feel you are a failure and become a part of the millions of Americans who are down and depressed.

I can assure you without any hesitation, without any exception, everyone can be a success. This is what I mean: You can succeed as a person, even if you do not succeed professionally. We must have a definition, of

*U.S. News & World Report, Sept. 9, 1974 (pg. 38)

course, of *success*. By success we do not mean that you have a multimillion dollar income. We are not measuring success now, in terms of dollars, status, fame or fortune.

Many years ago, when Dr. Beckering was a pastor in Chicago, Illinois, he was asked to make a call on the husband of one of the women of his congregation. This man, who was sick in his hospital bed, turned out to be a great nationally known physician in his own right. Dr. Beckering thought to himself, "What can I say to this great doctor, who now is on his bed with a nearfatal heart attack?"

When Dr. Beckering went into the room, the patient saw him and said, "Dr. Beckering, I'm glad to see you. Since I've been a patient myself here, I've had a revelation. The revelation, Dr. Beckering, is that it is not what you do in life that counts, it is what you are. I've done a lot, but I'm not the person I should have been."

It's not what you do, but what you are! He became, and is today, a fantastic Christian!

Which reminds me of what Goethe said, "Before you can do something, you have to be somebody." That means you have to *be* a beautiful person before you can *do* anything beautiful.

It's not what you do, it's what you are that counts. In that light, we can define success: *A beautiful person is a successful person, so beautiful people are never failures.* They may lose, but they do not fail. You can love and lose, but you cannot love and fail, for when you love you are beautiful.

I once did some research on several of the capitalists

who made America great. I had become interested in them because of the problem of inflation that we have in our country.

I found that Andrew Carnegie, who in his lifetime made a half billion dollars, made a profound statement. He said, "It's impossible to get rich without doing a lot of good for a lot of people." Now that was his attitude! Do you know what his goal was? Carnegie's goal was to bring the price of steel down from $160 a ton to $20 a ton, and he did it!

I also did some research on Henry Ford. Do you know what his burning desire was? His burning desire was to produce an automobile and do it well enough and cheap enough so that every American family could afford an automobile in their garage.

I studied a man named Gillette. He wanted to make it possible for every man to have a clean shave *cheap!*

And there was a man named Ingersoll who liked watches. When he was a young man he couldn't afford one. His goal was to produce watches for $1 so every man could have a watch in his pocket.

The greatest capitalists in American history made millions because their attitudes were not to make millions but to do a lot of good for a lot of common people. And with that attitude capitalism came very close to achieving the goal that socialists have proposed, namely, abundance for all in a classless society.

And now inflation threatens our country, and do you know why? I'm going to suggest something. Inflation is threatening the very life of capitalism because the *attitude* has changed in too many corporations (both in labor and in management) to "How can we get the most for ourselves," instead of "How can we do the most good for the most people." If that attitude dominates for long then capitalism will die, because everybody will try to get all they can for themselves; that will feed inflation which can kill our system.

So how do you change people's attitudes? By getting love inside! When you get a love for people as *persons*, when you're focused on service and not on self, you produce success.

Carnegie was right. Nobody is going to get rich and keep his riches unless he does a lot of good for a lot of people.

Love never fails, but selfishness always ultimately is suicidal. Get love inside, and you will be a successful person.

I said to an old woman, who was over seventy and under a hundred, "You are so beautiful."

She looked at me and said, "Well, I ought to be. I've lived with Him," and her eyes looked up to her Lord, "for eighty years."

Love never fails to produce successful, beautiful people.

Archibald Rutledge tells of a captain of one of the ships on the Mississippi River. One day the captain went to the engine room which was always spotlessly clean. As you know, engine rooms are usually the greasiest, dirtiest places on a ship. The captain said to the engineer, "Why is your engine room always so clean?"

And the man said, "Well, Captain, it's like this: I got a glory inside of me!"

Once there was a man who came onto the grounds of our church, stubbled beard, drunk, an outcast. The law came looking for him and caught him. They put him in jail. From his cell, a half mile east, he could see the cross on top of our Tower of Hope. He made contact with the lay people of this church, and they loved him and told him he could be saved, he could be born again, he could be literally transformed, changed, made into a different, new human being. And he believed it, and he accepted Jesus Christ.

What a conversion! So our church vouched for him. We gave him a job to clean up the place. He not only cleaned up the place, he went out and bought some paint and painted our engine room. You should see it! Every pipe is painted, every nut is painted, every washer is painted, every cable is painted, every engine is painted, every motor is painted, and the ceiling is painted blue with white stars. Purple, red, green, blue, orange, lavender, pink — you can't imagine how such a conglomeration of every color in the rainbow and a dozen more can be put into that one room, and it looks gorgeous! It's absolutely the most beautiful engine room in any place in the world!

I asked him, "Why did you paint it this way?"

"Because," he said, "that's the way I feel inside, since Jesus Christ came in."

You can live beyond the possibility of failure by becoming a beautiful person. You can become a beautiful person by taking Christ into your life. When that happens, LOVE will dominate your personality. And love never fails! So any person can be a great success personally if he'll simply turn his life over to Jesus Christ.

So my question is not how many dollars you have, not how much status you have, not how famous you are nor what position you have. My question is, Do you have Jesus Christ in your life?

·5·

Here's a Love to End Your Loneliness

*"So faith, hope, love abide, these three;
but the greatest of these is love."*
I COR. 13:13

I offer to you Jesus Christ.
Take Him and you'll have
an end to loneliness.

I HAVE FOR YOU an answer to what is undoubtedly one of the biggest problems in the world today, and that is the problem of *loneliness.*

Standing in my pulpit recently, addressing a full church, was a friend of mine who watches "Hour of Power" from her home in Minneapolis, Minnesota. Many of you know her as Dear Abby, whose column appears in over 900 newspapers. She said to me, "Dr. Schuller, loneliness, and the need for love that goes with it, is the number one problem that faces people." She told me she receives over 10,000 letters a week, and we receive that many ourselves. We both agreed that it is man's hunger for acceptance and understanding that is, of all needs, deepest.

Here is God's answer to the problem of loneliness:

"So faith, hope, love abide, these three;
but the greatest of these is love."
I COR. 13:13

Why is love greater than anything else? Because love alone meets man's deepest need, woman's deepest need and a child's deepest need, and that need is to be accepted where we are, as we are.

Loneliness is a battle that takes place between two persons who live inside of you within your soul. No person is so integrated that he is only one self. But deep within us there are many conflicting persons. Life is a crew of people within us, struggling to take over the helm.

Look at these two people within you: There is one person reaching out for love, like a little child in a candy store grasping for candy. This person reaches out desperately, anxiously, almost hysterically, for love and understanding. But there is another self who, like a father holding back a child's hand in a candy store, says to your grabbing self, "Look out! Don't grab so fast. You might get hurt. You might be rejected. You might not be accepted. You don't want to love and be rejected, do you?"

Love is a risky business, you know. To love is to be vulnerable. To be vulnerable is to be accountable. To be accountable is to run the risk of being rejected. To

be rejected you run the risk of all risks, and that is that
you might end up hating yourself because others don't
love you.

And so the lonely person is the one who listens ultimately to fear instead of to faith. The lonely person
is somebody who listens finally to the self that says, "Be
careful. Don't take any chances. Don't make any commitments. Don't get involved. You might get rejected.
You might get hurt." And if that's the voice you listen
to, you will have your freedom intact, but the price you
pay for your freedom from involvement is loneliness.

One reason our society is so infected with loneliness
is because the spirit of selfish freedom has become so
widespread. We don't want to risk losing our freedom
by getting involved. We don't want to lose our freedom
by running the risks of making the long-term commitments. So there are those who say, "What's the use of
marriage? It's only a piece of paper. Live together, love
together." And if the relationship cools you can split,
you can go your way, and nobody will get hurt. The
fallacy of that is that the man loves the girl only as long
as she's young. And then when the wrinkles come, he
deserts her. And when she's old, nobody cares, because
she sold herself too cheaply.

We have a lot of lonely people today because the
price of unwillingness to make permanent commitments is to live on a level of interpersonal relationships
where all relationships are temporary. When you are
hurt, like infantile children who pack up their marbles,
you can go your way and find yourself free again. But
remember, one day you may land in the hospital for

major surgery and discover that nobody knows, and nobody cares! Unless you are willing to surrender some freedom to make permanent commitments, prepare to pay the price: *loneliness.*

Love ends loneliness, but love has a price tag. The price tag of love is commitment to continuity. Like I said to a young couple the other day, "What makes marriage more important than a piece of paper? *One thing,* and that is when you say, 'I love you and always will love you, even when your skin is wrinkled.' That's when you're going to need it more than ever."

There are all kinds and forms of loneliness. "The Loneliness of Sinking," "The Loneliness of Suffering," "The Loneliness of Struggling," "The Loneliness of Striving," "The Loneliness of Searching," "The Loneliness of Succeeding," and finally, "The Loneliness of Sinning." Where do you fit in? Let's look at some of them:

The Loneliness of Sinking. Failure, of course, brings its own loneliness. Because when things aren't going right and you're facing bankruptcy, or your marriage is falling apart, and you have that sinking, failing feeling, you have a loneliness because you don't want to share your failure with others. You'd rather not talk about your failures! Nobody wants to hear a loser cry. (Except—it strikes me all of a sudden—that's one thing that is unique about Jesus Christ: He always has time to listen to a loser cry!)

The Loneliness of Succeeding. I don't know which is the worst. I have known the Loneliness of Sinking. There were two years in this ministry when the will to die was stronger than the will to live. I had dreams of a church with fountains and grounds where people could worship in their cars and inside the sanctuary. I had the whole vision. God showed me a tower with 24-hour telephone counseling and a staff of great ministers and a thousand more lay people like you who would do Christ's work. The whole dream was there. And the problems were monumental. I was sure I was failing. I know the Loneliness of Sinking. And I've known the Loneliness of Succeeding. For when you succeed, who wants to listen to you? With whom do you dare share your victories? Most people will think you're boasting! So there is the Loneliness of Success as well as the Loneliness of Sinking.

The Loneliness of Struggling. This is the time when you don't know if you're sinking or succeeding. You only know you're struggling! And you don't want to publicly admit you have problems. You don't want to show weakness; you don't want to expose imperfection. You want to hopefully keep a strong front.

You might remember hearing somewhere years ago someone utter a ghastly negative sentence that said, "Even rats flee from sinking ships." So you don't want to expose the fact that you've got problems.

Well, the truth is, every person in this world has problems. As Dr. Peale said in this pulpit one day, "Everybody has problems. The only person who doesn't have problems is dead. Anybody who is alive, really alive, has problems." Of course I would add: Anyone who is alive is getting involved. And a person who is getting in-volved is taking risks. And a person who is taking risks is living on the edge of nerve; he's taking a chance, and that's what makes him alive instead of dead with boredom.

The Loneliness of Striving. What do you do when you strive? God gives you a dream. Do you dare to tell peo-ple? It takes a lot of courage to love. It doesn't take much courage to hate, but it takes a lot of courage to love. There is the fear of what people will say, especially if we think big. Will they laugh and say, "Who do you think you are that you can be that person? Who do you think you are that you could amount to something? Boy, has something gone to your head! Wow, are you an egomaniac!" The fear of ridicule drives us to isolation which results in the Loneliness of Striving.

There is not infrequently an understandable fear that your ideas and your plans might be stolen by someone else. And you have to be protective of your concepts, until at least you have an option or a copyright or a patent. Meanwhile there's the Loneliness of Striving and Struggling and Succeeding and Sinking.

The Loneliness of Searching. Who has not known this searching between the choices; searching for the alter-natives; searching until you make the decision. Ulti-mately you alone make most of the decisions in your life. Ultimately you live alone. Peripheral living is cor-porate living, but solitary living is ultimate living. Let me explain.

64

For the most part, most of us live in interpersonal relationships; acting, reacting, responding, answering to the questions and the challenges and the instincts and the impulses of people around us. But that's peripheral living. Peripheral living is collective (or corporate) living. But ultimate living is solitary living. By that I mean that the ultimate life you live, you live alone. You were born alone. Maybe you had a twin, but both of you were born individually. You were born alone. When you learned to walk, you learned to walk alone. When you learned to talk, you learned to talk alone. True, there were those who guided, supported and sustained you. But you did it alone!

When you make the great decisions—what career or profession to follow, who to marry—only *you* make these decisions! Nobody else makes the decisions. Your father doesn't make them, your mother doesn't make them, your brother or sister doesn't make them. You do!

And ultimately when you accept or reject Jesus Christ, you make that decision. I do not make it for you. Your wife or your husband does not make it for you. Your father or mother does not make it for you. Your pastor or your church does not make it for you. You cannot cop out. You, and you alone, make that decision.

Peripheral living is corporate living, but ultimate living is solitary living.

And finally there comes the time when you die, and that is a moment alone. There will be those who will stand around you. They may be supportive and they

may be helpful. But you go alone. All alone. Unless you
have a very special friend.

Dr. Glasser, whose book, *Reality Therapy,* has been
helpful to many people, has a sentence that I find very,
very significant. He says, "Every man needs one essential friend." I would add: If you've got that, then you've
got a cure for loneliness.

I friend

And what do we mean? We mean that every person
should have one friend who is so intimate that he can
expose himself completely to him without making himself vulnerable, without fear that someday he'll tell or
he'll be exposed.

very good

Where can you find a friend you can trust like that?
I have such a friend. His name is Jesus Christ. He is
that one essential friend. I can go to Him and confess
all my sins, of thought, word and deed, and know that
He will put His arm around my shoulder and love me
anyway.

I can go to Him in the Loneliness of Striving and
He won't put me down. I can go to Him in the Loneliness of Searching for alternatives and ask His advice!
I can go to Him in the Loneliness of Struggling and
Sinking and be encouraged. I can go to Him in the
Loneliness of Succeeding and He will sense my joy. He
is the one essential friend who really cures loneliness,
for He offers a love that is deep and true and beautiful
and lasting, and it never lets you down.

We have beautiful flowers on these grounds. The other
day I stopped, for the first time, at the place where we
buy these flowers. There I met one of the most remark-

66

able people in my life. She's an old lady. When I went into the shop I saw her sitting behind the counter. She had her wrinkled old elbows on the glass. Her whole face was so wrinkled. Her hair was silver, and it was done with little hand curls in a very homey way. She had glasses on, perched at the tip of her old nose.

I went to the desk and she immediately said, "Oh, I want to tell you how much I enjoy you on television. I have some friends who go to a Bible church, and they say, 'Dr. Schuller doesn't preach Bible. He just preaches possibility thinking.'" And she shook a bony finger at the invisible friends. "But I say to them, 'There's possibility thinking in Scripture.'"

"God bless you," I said.

"Yes, it's Scripture," she continued. "Oh, it's done wonders for me. We came out here from Kansas, my husband and I. Then my husband passed away."

"I suppose you're lonely," I commented.

She jolted to attention and stood upright. "Lonely? I don't get lonely around here. There's always a new flower blooming every day."

She went on, "When the first cyclamen blooms they come running in here and bring it to me! Isn't it pretty?" She was so excited. "Loneliness," she said, "what is it? What is it?"

"You're a Christian, aren't you?" I asked.

"Oh, yes," she said. "I sure am, Dr. Schuller. I was converted in a little country church in Kansas when I was a young girl. I can show you the very spot and the very pew where I was saved. And Jesus has been my friend ever since."

neat

I looked at her face. It was beautiful for all her wrinkles were happy wrinkles. There wasn't one wrinkle that wasn't carved from a smile or from laughter.

She reminded me of my dad who passed away some years ago at the age of 83. I never knew my dad to experience loneliness. That man had the enormous capability of enjoying solitude without ever getting lonely. He knew how to live in those ultimate moments of solitary isolation with strength, peace of mind, calmness and joy. And I learned more from him than I could ever share with you. As I look back on it, it was because he too had one essential friend.

My dad was a poor man all his life on our Iowa farm, but he kept very busy. When he didn't work the fields, he was usually pounding and hammering in his woodshed or his toolshed. He had an old forge, an old anvil and a heavy hammer. Many times in his spare moments I would hear the ringing of the hammer echoing from the anvil. As a little boy I would run to the toolshed, and there would be the forge, red hot, and in it a red hot piece of iron. He would take it out, red and white hot, lay it on the anvil and crash down the heavy hammer, making an iron frame to hold a pot of blooming geraniums beside the house or a spare part to repair a broken piece of machinery.

But there was more than one time when the hammer was silent as I approached his place of work. I could hear my dad talking softly to his Friend, his God. Yes, so much like the old man in *Fiddler on the Roof.* I would hear him say, "I sure got myself a good-sized mortgage on this place. And we've got to work it out, don't we?"

You will never get lonely as long as there is one person who loves you with a love so great that you know you don't have to be a phoney around Him. You don't have to play games. You don't have to wear a mask. You don't have to pretend. He loves you anyway.

He will never condemn you. He will never scold you. He will never belittle you.

And the price? There is one price He demands—that you make a commitment to love Him forever. Yes, forever. That's the best deal you could ever have, because you will *want* Him forever.

What a friend we have in Jesus,
All our sins and griefs to bear.
What a privilege to carry
Everything to Him in prayer.

I offer to you Jesus Christ. Take Him and you'll have a love to end all loneliness.

·6·

"I Forgive You"— The Language of Love

"Love is not resentful."
I COR. 13:5

Resentments are snowdrifts
and forgiveness is
the snowplow.

ARE YOU CARRYING resentments? How many fears, how many anxieties, how many worries are you suffering from because you will not forgive somebody who hurt you deeply? How many sunny days are turned grey by your angry mind, seething, quarrelling in fantasy bouts with your adversary, an ex-husband, an ex-wife, a relative, a neighbor, a customer, a client or a clerk?

Are you suffering from ulcers or arthritis or high blood pressure or even heart problems because you will not forgive? And how many people are developing wrinkles in their skin that will become permanent creases, monuments to the fact that they spent most of their lives thinking angry thoughts, until the frown wrinkles work their way irreducibly into their countenance?

How many friends did you once have who now no longer talk to you because you developed a reputation of pouting, grumbling and complaining because you just couldn't handle the daily resentments that got under your skin?

This leads me to these words I want to share with you from I Corinthians 13, the great Love chapter:

"Love is not resentful."
I COR. 13:5

Born and raised in northwest Iowa, I can recall the first snow. It was wonderful. But what we didn't appreciate were the blizzards, because the blizzards would come in driving winds of 50 to 60 miles an hour until sometimes they closed the road with an impassable drift. We wouldn't be able to get out to the store to buy our food. It was serious. One positive thing was I wouldn't have to go to school! And then I remember we would look out of our farm house half mile down the road to the hill where we could see the snowplow coming, cutting through the drifts, slicing the snow, chopping it up and blowing it into a huge, spewing stream into a ditch. And when the snowplow came through, the road was open again, and we could go for our food. And I could go for my education.

Resentments are snowdrifts, and forgiveness is the snowplow. You see, forgiveness in the eyes of the non-

Christian is simply a matter of passive acquittal. But in the Christian context that's not it at all. In the Christian context forgiveness is the snowplow. It means opening the road, removing the barrier, so that you can now communicate and listen again to what people are trying to say. We dialogue and interchange; we move back and forth. Whether it's between my God and myself or a person and myself, forgiveness is a snowplow, not just an eraser on a blackboard.

There are a lot of resentments that build up in lives in a period of a day. And the only way to put joy on your face is to find an overpowering love that can remove them and fill you with forgiveness. "I forgive you," is the language of love.

Now, in order to conquer resentments, in order to submit to the forgiving spirit, let's understand what some of the obstacles are:

Obstacle #1: An extreme sense of justice. I have had a problem with this myself. I have a strong sense of justice. It seems to me that we have to remember what the word of God tells us: *"Vengeance is mine."* (Deut. 32:35)

I have often been helped by the story of Joseph. He was sold by his brothers as a slave to Egypt. They had hoped they could kill him and get him out of the way. He became, however, a ruler. They meant to kill him, and they ended up in the providence of God crowning him. As Joseph said, "You meant it for evil, but God meant it for good." Let justice be handled by the Lord. He knows how to take care of people.

There was a man who was the victim of injustice who

said to his pastor, "But wouldn't it be man-like of me to be angry?"

And his pastor said, "Indeed it would. But it would be Christ-like of you to forgive."

Obstacle #2: Making a mountain out of a molehill. We tend, you know, to emphasize the little negative things that get under our skin and forget all positive qualities. The person who has hurt you, no matter who he is, does have many fine qualities, but chances are you can't see them.

Once, to illustrate this point, I took before a class (I was teaching Possibility Thinking) a sheet of paper, 8 ½ × 11. I tacked it on a board, and with a felt pen I made a circle and a straight line on it. Then I asked members of my class to come up and tell me what they saw. One person said a line; another said a circle. Every person came up, and after the last person spoke I said, "Not one of you said, 'I see a sheet of paper.'" What I had tacked up was a sheet of white paper. All they saw were the black markings on it, they didn't see the mass of white.

We tend, by nature, to be negative thinkers. We see the wrong, and we don't see the good. That becomes an obstacle. We take a little detail and get hung up on it.

It's like an artist who was teaching his students how to paint. He took them out to paint a sunset. They set up their easels, and began to paint. Just as the sky was reaching its height of colorful glory, they noticed one student, who was lost in painting the shingles on a barn in the foreground of the pastoral scene. The teacher said, "Look, if you spend so much time painting the shingles, you will miss the sunset." Don't get so hung up on details that you miss the big picture.

Obstacle #3: Seeing the possibilities in the offensive experience. In other words, we forget all of the positive possibilities that are in an offensive situation. We forget that this, too, is the time when you can turn your scars into stars.

A few years ago I flew from Europe to a very prominent East Coast city where I was to deliver a Sunday morning sermon at a huge church. At the Geneva airport I had cashed my two $50 traveler's checks and received two $50 bills in exchange.

We arrived at our hotel the night before, and I noticed that a neighborhood theatre was showing a particular movie—a movie I had reason to believe might give me some good illustrations for my sermon.

So Mrs. Schuller and I went to the theatre. We stood in line, a long line, and we could see that the movie was starting in just a few minutes and I didn't want to miss the opening. Two minutes before the opening I was at the theatre window. I gave the ticket teller a $50 bill. She looked at it and said, "I'm sorry, we don't take $50 bills."

I said, "You can't reject it. Do you know what that bill says? It says, 'This is legal tender for all debts public and private.' You can't refuse it." (I had my tickets already.)

But she said, "I'm sorry, we can't take it."

Now, never in my life have I been a public protester,

77

but the line was getting longer and longer behind me and it was starting to drizzle. I said, "I'm sure you'll take it, because it's a good $50 bill."

She said, "I'm sorry, we won't take it." The line got longer, and I was getting impatient. Finally she said, "You've got your tickets."

"All right," I said, "thank you," and I walked in.

Then she stuck her neck out and yelled at the head usher, "That man didn't pay!"

I had a vast listening audience in this city, and I thought, "Oh, God, I hope nobody recognizes me."

The usher stopped me and asked, "What's the big idea?"

I told him, "She wouldn't take my $50 bill, and it's all I've got. I just left Geneva twelve hours ago, and I'm sorry. But you watch where I sit, and you just check with the hotel and see if there isn't a Robert Schuller listed there, and check out if they think he's honest or not. When I get out of the theatre, you'll have had time to check me out."

Unfortunately, halfway through the movie I had to step out to the men's room. I no sooner got in the men's room than there was that same usher standing right by me. "Okay," he said, "you are either the greatest counterfeit or the greatest con man I've ever met."

"Did you check the hotel?" I questioned.

"No," he said sternly, "I don't have to. I can spot a con man a mile off."

"Look," I said, "here is the $50 bill. You take it, check it out, and when I leave the theatre, give me $45 back please. I want to go in and watch the movie." And I left him with the $50 bill.

When the movie was over, I couldn't find the usher, but I saw a man in a black coat who looked like he was an official. I said to him, "I'm looking for the head usher. He's got my $50 bill."

He looked at me and said, "Oh, you're the guy with the $50 bill! We don't take $50 bills here."

"Well, I want my change, $45, or I want the $50 bill back," I persisted.

Then he reached into his pocket, and with a terrible look on his face he said, "Here is your blankety-blank $50 bill," and he threw it on the floor. So I reached down and picked it up and put it in my pocket. And do you know what? I was mad! Which is not a Christian emotion! Well, I prayed about it, but I was kind of offended.

We walked out of the theatre, and it was raining. We had to walk three blocks to the hotel. My wife said to me, "Bob, this is a great opportunity to practice what you preach. This is loaded with possibilities."

"It is?" I said. "Like what?"

"Well, let's go back to the hotel, we'll break the bill at the hotel, come back here, pay them the $5, and the usher will listen as we leave a witness for Jesus Christ."

We got to the hotel, got change for the $50 bill and walked back to the theatre through the rain. We knocked persistently at the closed door and just kept knocking until the girl who ran the peanut stand opened the door. "Not you again," she said.

"Please, can I see the head usher?" I asked.

I went in just in time to see the usher coming down the steps carrying his tuxedo. He was wearing his street clothes. "Oh my God, not you again," he protested.

I said, "Yes, it is me again. I have come to pay you the $5 I owe you."

"Oh, you didn't have to do that," he said.

"I did have to do it," I answered. "I owe it to you. But now you owe me something. I want you to know that I am doing this for one reason: I claim to be a Christian, and it's very exciting trying to follow Christ in daily life. I want you, for the rest of your life, to never forget that if you ever hear people say that Christians are all a bunch of hypocrites, that there's nothing to this Jesus Christ and God business. I want you never to forget that once a man you didn't know came in dripping wet out of the rain to pay his $5 because he said he was a Christian, and that makes a difference."

His eyes were moist. He took the $5 and said, "Yes, sir. Thank you, sir. Good night, sir. I'm very sorry." And we smiled and shook hands.

Do you know what it means to forgive? To forgive doesn't just mean that you erase the slate. Forgiveness means you cut the road open and you move back and forth and you help each other. You don't just acquit the person. You see their possibilities and you make them into something beautiful. That can happen to you. But it can only happen when Jesus Christ comes into your life.

I don't think anybody can live in today's world and

go through a day, to say nothing of a week or a month, without having the love of Christ in his heart to give the kind of forgiving power we must have today and tomorrow.

·7·

How You Can Have the Power to Cope

"Love endures all things."
I COR. 13:7

Keep on possibilitizing!

IT'S A FASCINATING thing to study human beings! As a minister-counselor-author I have specialized in this for nearly a quarter of a century. I can report to you that, under stress, human beings will usually react in one of four ways:

1. Some people will *mope* their way through their troubles. They quickly surrender to self-pity which gives rise to bitterness.

2. Other people *dope* their way through; they use narcotics from a bottle, a box, or a bag.

3. Lots of people just *grope* their way. They get so con-

fused they don't know where they're going. They lose sight of God's plan for their life. So they take their eye off their goal when they start groping.

4. And some people *hope.* In that hope they find *power to cope.* So they make it!

Now, how do you build your hope so that you can cope? I want to answer that in three words.

I was riding down the freeway the other day and I saw a sign on the back of a vehicle: a sign I have seen on the back of cars, and sweaters of kids in high school. It said, "Keep on Trucking." I really don't know what it means, but I'm going to give you three words that I'd like to make into a bumper sticker! My hope-building three words are: *"Keep on Possibilitizing."*

Do you know what that means? I don't know what trucking means, but I'll tell you what "possibilitizing" means! It is *imagining,* it is *visualizing,* it is *praying,* it is *multiplying* mentally, it is *overcoming,* it is *anticipating,* it is *toughening,* it is *maneuvering,* it is *rebounding* and it is *overpowering* the problem! Let's look at some of these points:

• *Possibilitizing is imagining.* When God's presence comes into your life through Jesus Christ, Love is going to come into you. This love will so overpower the negative thoughts that you will be able to possibilitize your way out of your situation. Possibilitizing is imagining that things are going to get better; they're not going to stay the way they are.

While lecturing in New York I placed a telephone

call to a young woman who told me how she had been transformed through our "Hour of Power" ministry. She said, "A year ago I had major surgery, and it didn't look like I'd live. I asked my doctor, 'Doctor, do you think I'll ever walk again?'

"He looked at me intently and said, 'That's the wrong question.'

"I said, 'I don't think so. I think that's the right question. Do you think I'll ever walk again?'

"And he answered, 'You're wrong and I'm right. The right question is not do *I* think you'll ever walk again, but do *you* think you'll ever walk again?'"

Problems really become serious when they get you to take your eye off your goal. Constantly imagine that things will get better. They're not going to stay the way they are. If you imagine they're going to get better, you will be in a frame of mind to contribute to their getting better instead of getting worse.

On a sundial in London, England, is this statement: "It's always morning somewhere in the world."

• *Possibilitizing is visualizing victory beyond the battle of the hour.* It's seeing the victory instead of the battle. It's seeing the ultimate reward instead of the pain. It's seeing the crown instead of the cross.

Wesley, that great Methodist minister, was once talking with a farmer friend out in the country. They saw a cow with her head over a stone wall, looking out into the distance. Wesley said to the farmer, "Suddenly I'm perplexed by a question. Why would that cow be looking over the wall?"

And the farmer answered, "Well, that's simple: she's looking over the wall because she can't look through it."

Again and again in your life you're going to have problems, setbacks, rejections, disappointments, discouragements and prayers that seemingly are not answered. God may not seem to be around. You may really hit low. You may even think that prayer doesn't work and God isn't real and Christ isn't real. You'll run into a stone wall. When you run into a stone wall and you can't cope, what do you do? *You look over it when you can't see through it!*

Keep on possibilitizing!

For years Steve Genter, from Lakewood, California, trained for the Munich Olympics. He wanted to win so badly in the 200-meter freestyle swim. Some of you may remember what happened. One week before the big event his lung collapsed, and they said that would wipe him out. But that isn't what he thought. He looked beyond the moment and over the wall! At his insistence they cut his chest open, repaired the lung and stitched him back up. When they called the names for the event in Munich, Germany, they called out the name of Steve Genter, and he came up, stitched and taped! One week after they cut his chest open, he stood there determined to still try.

He was in the 100-meter turn of the 200-meter freestyle event, in a neck-and-neck race with Mark Spitz, when he hit a dead wall, ripped his stitches open! It threw his timing off, but he kept swimming, and he came in seconds behind Mark Spitz! He came home from the Olympics with a gold medal, a silver medal and a bronze medal!

I've studied the human being and I can tell you that when he looks over the wall to the reward, he'll forget about the pain. Remember, Steve Genter could take no drugs and no medication because that's an Olympics law.

• *Possibilitizing is praying.* If God has control over your life, He will not let you quit, but He'll keep you in a possibilitizing mood which is praying: "Father, your will be done. This, too, will pass; it cannot last."

A listener to "Hour of Power" sent me this beautiful poem:

She used to say to me when things went wrong,
"Why make them worse with worry and regret?
Lift up your heart and join the merry throng
And in the rush of hope you will forget
Nothing is lasting in this changing sphere.
The troubles that now seem more than you
  can bear
Will all have vanished in another year
Like smoke that melts in the morning air."
And as I look back now across the years,
I know how very truthfully she spoke.
Time soothes our wounds and stays our falling
  tears,
And from our shoulders lifts the galling yoke.
No sorrow is as lasting as it seems.
The dark cloud that now obscures the gracious day

Will soon be severed by the sun's white beams
And in the glow of noon will fade away.

Keep on praying! After Good Friday comes Easter
morning!

• *Possibilitizing is multiplying the results.* Some of you are
tempted to quit because you don't see the returns and
the results. We've had Sunday School teachers quit because they didn't think they were doing a good job; they
couldn't see the results. I know of ministers who have
given up the ministry because they thought they were
failing. If only they would keep on possibilitizing! I
know salesmen who gave up because they thought they
were bombing out. What you should do is possibilitize.
That means mentally multiply the possible results!

We're getting ready as a church to celebrate our an-
niversary and we're planning fabulous things. I can go
back and remember when there was a period of two
years when it looked like nothing was happening and
everything was sinking. Failure was the only thing that
would come our way. But we kept visualizing and we
kept imagining and we kept praying, and in our minds
we kept multiplying what God could do!

I was inspired by the story of George Smith, the
Moravian missionary. All his life he wanted to be a missionary to Africa. He finally finished his preparation
and traveled to Africa. He was there but a few months
when he was expelled. When he was expelled he left
behind only one convert, an old woman. He came back
home and soon died, still a young man, literally on his

knees praying for Africa, for the people he had come
to love. Think of it! All of his life he was preparing . . .
he went there . . . spent only a few months . . . came
home and died a very young man! But one hundred
years later that mission of one old woman had grown
into 13,000 happy Christians!

Any fool can count
the seeds in an apple,
but only God can count
the apples in a seed.

Possibilitizing—multiply what's going to happen! Now
you can cope when you can imagine that something
good will ultimately happen. *So keep on possibilitizing!*

• *Possibilitizing is overcoming* rather than allowing yourself to be overcome.

Earlier I told you about Pat Shaughnessy. Pat is one
of the ministers who has been inspired by our possibility thinking. Pat was at a ticket counter when a bomb
went off and killed three people. He suddenly found
himself without his leg, blasted off near the hip.

When I called him in the hospital, I asked him how
he was doing. He laughed at the other end of the line
and said, "It's fantastic how God doesn't let anything
happen to us unless it's great!"

He went on, "You know, Bob, losing a leg isn't that
bad. I'm sure people who have never had it happen
would say it's impossible to live without a leg. But you
know, it isn't so bad. I've got my brain. And I've got my

mental attitude straightened out. And guess what? In two weeks I'm going back into the pulpit again, after an absence of nearly three months. I don't know if I'll be preaching in my wheelchair or sitting on a stool, but I'm going to be back, and it's going to be the greatest Sunday in the history of our church."

I asked him, "What's the key? What's the real reason you can have such a positive attitude?"

And he said, "When you've got Jesus Christ in your heart, then everything else is so exciting that all of the problems you have are really unimportant." So . . .

• *Possibilitizing is anticipating* that good will come out of adversity.

Betty Ford, President Ford's wife, said when she went through her surgery, "I'm confident and secure and relaxed, because I believe that God will use this to do a lot of good for a lot of people." And there are a lot of women today who will not die of cancer because they had their examination after Betty Ford had her surgery.

That's what we call anticipating. In the book of Romans, written by Paul, it says, *"We know that in everything God works for good with those who love him, who are called according to his purpose."* (Rom. 8:28)

• *Possibilitizing is toughening yourself.* It's keeping up the exercise, it's keeping up the preparation, it's keeping up the training, it's keeping up the working, it's keeping up the studying, it's keeping up the road work: Being tough on yourself. That's what possibilitizing is. We've never said that possibility thinking makes success cheap and easy. I will tell you this, *no success ideas will work if you don't.*

Now, how do you motivate yourself to keep going in the tough times? Well, let me tell you what has helped me.

I am in a running program, and this morning I frankly didn't feel like running. I thought to myself, "I'll skip today. After all, I've got a full day's work. I have to preach a couple of services and I've some things to do this afternoon and a big meeting tonight, so I think I'll just skip the running today because I really don't feel like it." Then this thought struck me: "All you have to do to be a lasting success is to do what you should when you don't feel like it! If you will do what you should do when you don't feel like it, you'll be doing it all the time because you'll surely do it when you feel like it!" So I went out and ran four miles this morning.

Possibilitizing and possibility thinking is toughening yourself.

I almost never buy clothes. My wife selects most of my clothes, because I don't have the time or the inclination to shop and I'm not that interested in clothes. But I needed a new coat, so I stopped in a store that had a half-price sale going on. That kind of motivated me. I went into the shop and saw what I thought was a beautiful coat. It was a green and white plaid. It sounds shocking, I know, but I thought it was nice. I picked out a pair of green pants to go with it, but I think I was looking at the half price more than the match. The owner of the shop said to me, "You know, the green pants don't quite do it." Then he made this statement: "And it would be a pity to miss it when you're so close." So he put the green pants away.

I looked through the whole pile of half-price pants, and I found another pair. I said, "This looks pretty good, don't you think?"

"No," the owner said, "it really doesn't. I must say, it's a pity to miss it when you're so close."

Then he went through the racks of men's pants that weren't on sale! He picked one out, laid it alongside the green coat and said, "You know, it still doesn't quite do it." So he put the pants back.

I said, "How about black? Doesn't black go with everything?"

"Oh, I wouldn't like black with it," he replied.

And the next thing I knew he took that beautiful green and white plaid sport coat and put it back on the rack and said, "Sorry, I won't sell it to you. I don't have the pants to go with it, and I wouldn't sell it to you if it wouldn't be right."

I walked out of there, and all I could think of was what he had said, *"It would be a pity to miss it if you come so close."*

Many of you are tempted to quit. Well, don't give up. *Don't quit when you're so close.* Some of you still, for instance, have one step to take before you have success. I'm thinking of some of you spiritually. Wouldn't it be a tragedy to come to the end of your life and have somebody say about you: "It's a pity that he missed it. He came so close! He quit just before he would have made it!"

The real power behind possibilitizing is the power from God Himself that comes into a human life when that life accepts Jesus Christ as its Saviour and Lord. And some of you have not done that. Simply receive Christ into your life by faith. He's alive. He can change you.

He lives within me. I have a relationship with Him. I know He has saved me from my sins. I know the worst that could happen is I'd die. But when that happens I will be born again into eternal life, because He's my Saviour. I've come so close and I won't miss it, because He will never let me down. He won't let you down, either.

Do you want to have power to cope? Get Christ's love in your life, because God's love is the love that endures all things.

Saint Paul did it. He received Christ into his life and amazing power came in! *"I can do all things through Christ who strengthens me."* (Phil. 4:13)

Listen: If you never have before—then this moment receive Christ into your life. Feel His love flow in. Feel the Spiritual Power! You'll start moving . . . you'll pos-sibilitize! You'll overcome!

·8·

Love Conquers Fear

"There is no fear in love."
I JOHN 4:18

You need me,
therefore I love you.
This is Christian love

WOULDN'T IT BE wonderful if something happened deep within your mind to give you such inner confidence, security and calmness that you would never be afraid of anybody or anything ever again? Wouldn't it be fantastic if you had a mental and spiritual experience that would permanently give you an imperishable and invisible shield against anxiety, worry, fear and guilt? The truth is, if you have an experience with Perfect Love, you will conquer fear in your life *forever*.

> *"There is no fear in love, for perfect*
> *love casts out fear."*
> I JOHN 4:18

What is very important is that we understand that there is such a thing as *imperfect* love and there is such a thing as *perfect* love. All doctrines, all lectures, all sermons, all messages, all books, all songs that talk about love are imperfect. And that's part of our problem in the world today. Much of what we think of as love is imperfect love. Consider this: There are three levels of love:

Level #1: "I love you because I need you." This is imperfect love. It is basically selfish.

Level #2: "I love you because I want you." This may be nothing more than lust.

Level #3: "I love you because you need me." I need to give myself away to people who need help. You need me, therefore I love you." This is Christian love.

Look at these three statements and you will see the difference between counterfeit and authentic love; between imperfect and perfect love.

"I need to give myself away to people who need help. You need me, therefore I love you." This is the essence of perfect love. Where do you find it?

Once I passed through one of our great mid-America airports. I had just delivered a lecture at a college where they required all the students on the campus to read my book entitled, *Self-Love, the Dynamic Force of Success.* I was asked to deliver a lecture on the subject, and answer questions from the student body. It was one of those quick 24-hour, out-of-town trips. As I was returning through this airport I stopped, as I often do, at a candy store. It was a Fannie Mae candy store.

I must hasten to say that I don't like candy. I used to like it, but I have psyched myself out because I've decided that the only way to lose weight is not to diet. Do you know what a diet is? A diet is when you deprive yourself of something you want to reach an objective, at which point you reward yourself by giving yourself what you've denied yourself all the time. So I decided the only way to lose weight, and keep it off, was to lose my appetite for foods that would make me fat. So I programmed myself (I think) not to like candy. I tell myself that the chocolate is either too bitter or it's too ghastly sweet. And if that doesn't work I imagine that their creamy contents were probably put together under unsanitary conditions.

At any rate, I go through this whole mental rigmarole to convince myself that I can't stand candy. But I stopped in to buy chocolates for my wife; she loves chocolates. She happens to particularly love chocolate-covered nuts. So I walked into this Fannie Mae store where a clerk in a white dress greeted me from behind the counter. There was another customer at the counter, an older woman, in a red dress with a flight bag and a little suitcase. She seemed to be indecisively window shopping.

The woman in white wasn't doing anything to help her, so I said, "Do you have one-pound boxes of chocolate-covered nuts?"

And at that point the customer said, "Oh, sure they've got one-pound boxes of all kinds of chocolate-covered nuts."

I looked back at the clerk who was after all the real authority. She could see that I was waiting for her to answer. "Yes, we can make up a one-pound box of all kinds of chocolate-covered nuts."

"Maybe you have a one-pound box of turtles, chocolate-covered nuts with caramel?" I asked.

The customer interrupted again, "Yes, they have those in one-pound boxes. They also have those in three-pound boxes!"

I looked at the clerk, waiting for the reply from the real authority (not content with the doubtful opinion of just another plain customer!) The clerk looked nervously at the customer who kept interrupting and finally said, "Yes, we do have them in one-pound boxes. We also have them in three-pound boxes."

Again she looked nervously at the customer. And again this customer intruded with the unsolicited advice: "But I recommend you take the one-pound box of the Colonial. It's got creams in it, too!"

The clerk on the other side of the counter said, "Yes, why don't you try the one with the creams? The Colonial is really a very good box!"

I thought to myself, "Who is working for whom around here?" It really became quite exasperating. "How much is the Colonial box?" I asked.

The clerk told me how much it was, and then the customer came back and said, "Really, their Colonial box has got everything. It's got chocolate turtles, chocolate-covered nuts, cashews, walnuts and peanuts," adding enthusiastically, "they're beautifully packaged, too!" Just then she said, "Oh, I've got to go or I'll miss my plane," and she picked up her bag and left. Both the clerk and I breathed sighs of relief to see her leave.

Immediately the clerk in the white dress turned around and called, "Okay, girls, you can come out now. Fannie Mae is gone!"

"You're kidding!" I gasped.

"Oh, no," she said. "That's Fannie Mae. Well, that's not her real name, but when her husband died and left her the candy store, she decided she was going to make something of her life. She put together some new recipes and packaged some new candies and now has one hundred seventeen stores all up and down the United States! She calls them her one hundred seventeen children, and all she does is fly around to visit the stores."

She was the authority, and I wasn't even listening to her! She knew the recipes, she put the whole thing together, and I was foolishly looking to some clerk as the authority—a clerk who probably never made a chocolate in her life!

If you want to know about love, then listen to the real authority, Jesus Christ! Ministers, priests and psychologists at best are clerks. We can only take the concept and give it to you. But we don't manufacture it! We don't create it. All the while, maybe through sermons, songs or people who write literature, Jesus Christ is coming to you, and you consider Him an intruder and are vastly relieved when He gets out and leaves you alone. Go to the authority! The real authority is Jesus Christ. He is perfect love!

"Perfect love casts out fear." Christ is perfect love. In other words, when Jesus Christ comes into your life, I won't have to tell you what love is. You will know from

personal experience! And that's the only way to know. There is a hymn that closes with the lines, "The love of Jesus, what it is, none but His loved ones know." It's not something you can be *taught,* it has to be *caught.*

I like the lesson I learned from Frank Laubach: "None of us loves perfectly, but Christ loves perfectly. No human being is totally perfect in love, but Christ is. Now, let's suppose you run into somebody you can't love. What do you do? Do you let yourself hate them? No. Do you tell yourself, 'I'm a Christian, therefore I'm going to love them'? Yes. Tell yourself that, *but it might not work.* Be realistic. What do you do? Surrender to your negative thoughts about the person? Of course not. You call in the expert, the authority, Jesus Christ."

Here's how Laubach taught us how to handle the situation: "Put one hand up in the air, open your palm and stretch the other hand out with a pointed finger aimed at your adversary. Now pray: 'Jesus Christ, you are perfect love. I am imperfect love. Because I'm imperfect I can't love that guy.' (Keep your finger pointed right at him! Aim at his heart. Aim at his head.) Pray: 'Jesus Christ, will you please fall into the palm of my hand, flow down through my arm, through my elbow, through my shoulder, my chest, my heart, down my other arm, out of the end of my finger, and hit him, please? Hit him hard! Hit him gently! Hit him beautifully! You love him, Jesus! You can do it! I can't do it! But *you* can!'"

I gave that lesson some years ago in this church. One man who heard me thought to himself: "Boy, Schuller's getting carried away again." He said to me a week later,

"Dr. Schuller, guess what happened? Monday morning I went to work remembering your sermon of the day before. The first person I saw coming into my store was the one salesman I could not stand! I saw him drive up to the curb; I knew his car. I saw him get out of that car. And I was already in a bad mood! My secretary, who also goes to this church and heard the same sermon I heard, said to me, 'Maybe you'd better try what Dr. Schuller talked about yesterday. Shoot him with prayers.' So before he got in I reached one hand in the air and with the other hand I pointed at him through the window. He was gawking at me as if I was nuts.

"Later on he told me he thought I was going to change a light bulb. But I said, 'Jesus, I can't love that guy. I can't stomach him, to say nothing of loving him. But *you* can. Flow into my hand, through my arm, through my heart, and *you* love him, Jesus.' And the most amazing thing happened. I couldn't believe it. When the man came up to me and said, 'Good morning. How are you today?'—and I've never heard him say it that way before— I looked at his face and saw that it had a countenance about it that I never saw before. His eyes, that always looked so nasty, now looked so sweet. It worked! *I ended up loving this guy!*"

"Perfect love casts out fear." It casts out all kinds of negative forces. Perfect love is Christ flowing through you. Christ is perfect love. So the secret, of course, is to have a personal relationship with Christ. And this is possible!

Why does it cast out fear? For one simple reason: Selfish love always produces fear. If I love you because I need you, or I love you because I want you, I'm going to be afraid that I might not get you, and then I'll have lost something that I wanted to gain. But if you love because you want to give something to somebody, you'll never become fearful or worried or tense. For *a giving love can never lose:* If they take what you offer, you'll succeed! . . . and if they don't take it, you've still got it! Either way, *you can't lose!* So there will be no subliminal anxieties or fears of being rejected or hurt.

Selfish love is the kind of love that builds walls more than it builds bridges.

It reminds me of what Robert Frost once wrote,

Before I built a wall I'd ask to know
What I was walling in or walling out

I was in St. Louis, Missouri, where I was to give a lecture. It was four o'clock in the afternoon, and I was to give my lecture in the main hall that night. So I unpacked my suitcase and pulled out the grey suit that I was going to wear for my lecture, just to make sure it was in good shape. Then I made this discovery: I hadn't worn the suit for four months and in the meantime I had lost 36 pounds. So the trousers were way too big for me. Unfortunately, they were trousers that didn't have loops for a belt.

Now you talk about being nervous! To be a lecturer on a platform in a pair of pants that are a 42 when you wear a 38! — I had a problem! I knew I either had to get a very hefty safety pin or I needed some emergency tailoring done in a hurry. I called the desk in the hotel. They told me no tailor could do it in such a short time.

But they said, "You can always go to Mr. Harris. Maybe he could do it."

So I went down to Harris the Tailor in the mall in downtown St. Louis, three blocks away. There I met one of the most marvelous of men, Mr. Harris, a seasoned gentleman, who really knew his business.

"Sir, can you take my trousers in about four inches?" I asked.

"Well, that'll take about two hours," he answered.

I looked him right in the eye and said, "Sir, aren't you Mr. Harris?"

"Yes," he said.

I continued, "I was told you're the best tailor in town."

"Well, ah, . . . " he hesitated.

I went on, "I happen to know a tailor in Los Angeles who could do it in twenty minutes. And I'm sure you're better than he is."

He just stared at me. And I stared at him, because I needed the job done. He finally said, "Okay, go to that little room there and throw me your trousers."

I walked into the room, carrying a book I had just bought, when Mr. Harris asked, "What's the name of that book you've got?"

Loneliness, the Fear of Love, I told him.

"Well, you're going to get awful lonely in there waiting for these pants to get done," he said.

"Oh, I don't think I'll get lonely," I replied. "I never get lonely, because I've got a friend who is with me."

Seventeen minutes later my trousers were back with the best job of tailoring I've ever seen!

"Are you a minister or something?" Mr. Harris asked.

"You look a little familiar."

"Yes, sir, I am," I told him.

"What kind of religion do you have? What is your faith?" he asked.

"I'm glad you asked that, Mr. Harris," I said. "What does my faith mean to me? Well, it's not a *religion*. By that I mean simply a course like psychology, sociology, anthropology, biology or chemistry. It's not a religion — like some spiritual kind of philosophy.

"And it's not a set of *restrictions:* Don't do this, don't do that. And it's not a list of *resolutions:* I'm going to do this, I'm going to do that. And it's not a *ritual:* Now we pray, now we bow our heads, now we give the offering. Now we read the Bible.

"No, my faith is a *relationship.* I have a friend, and He's Jesus Christ! I have received Him into my life, and I feel that within myself there is a Love that never leaves me. That's a love that conquers my fear. I'm not afraid to die tonight, because I know that I won't go to hell, I'll go to heaven. I have a Saviour. So the ultimate fear is flushed out! Because He died on a cross for me and He has scars to prove it!"

I invite you now to receive Jesus Christ into your life by faith. Then a Love will come into your life that will give you amazing peace of mind! And when that happens you've really found the answer to a love that drives out loneliness forever.

Love or loneliness . . . you decide!

Choose love — by choosing to receive Jesus Christ into your life . . . NOW!